A FIELD GUIDE
TO
FLY FISHING

A FIELD GUIDE TO FLY FISHING

DENNIS BITTON

Illustrated by
ROD WALINCHUS

THE LYONS PRESS
Guilford, Connecticut
An imprint of The Globe Pequot Press

The Lyons Press is an imprint of The Globe Pequot Press.

10 9 8 7 6 5 4 3 2 1

Printed in the United States of America

ISBN 1-59228-307-1

Frontispiece: *A duo of recently landed jack crevalle. (See page 115 for description.)*

Cover Illustration by Rod Walinchus.

All color photography by R. Valentine Atkinson/Frontiers.

Illustrated by Rod Walinchus, Livingston, Montana.

Library of Congress Cataloging-in-Publication Data is available on file.

CONTENTS

LEFTY'S PREFACE

Knowledge leads to success. The better we understand a subject, the more success we can achieve in it. This also applies to fly fishing.

Chances are, someday you will fish for a species you've never caught before. A book that gives identification pointers and information on the life history of your quarry can be fun reading. It pays to find out exactly what fish look like, where they live, and what conditions will work for or against you when you fly fish for them. Fishing tips — that bluefish require a fly on a wire bite leader, for example, or that billfish should be offered a fly which is no more than nine inches long — are important types of things to know to help you score better.

This field guide discusses the 51 fresh and saltwater fish that I think over time have become recognized as the principal gamefish for the fly rod. But neither the author, Dennis Bitton, nor I would claim this little book was the fish encyclopedia to end all fish encyclopedias. (For all types of fishing, not just fly fishing, there is already one of those, and a superb one it is. *McClane's New Standard Fishing Encyclopedia and International Angling Guide,* edited by my old friend, the late A.J. McClane, and published by Holt, Rinehart and Winston, New York, 1974. Al's massive work, with over 6,000 entries, 1,100 pages, and an extensive bibliography, is the standard reference work. Fly fishing is just a small part of this huge volume. It also covers bait casting, deep-sea fishing, surf casting, spinning, spin casting, trolling, bottom fishing, and commercial fishing; famous fishing authors and scientists; international angling; ecology; marine biology, including fish diseases and parasites; nearly 1,500 fish, in detailed descriptions; and much, much more. Every fishing writer and editor I know owns a copy, as do thousands of people who have a serious interest in the marine life of the world. If you share that interest and don't have a copy of *McClane's*, you should.) Our guide does not pretend to cover the thousands of species, subspecies, and hybrids of fish that exist throughout the waters of the world. Heck, somewhere out there, I'll bet there's a fly fisherman taking a fish that Dennis and I have never even heard of!

Also, since this is not an encyclopedia, where it makes good sense we have chosen to group some species and subspecies together. Take panfish, for example. You will see we have chosen the bluegill to represent all the panfish species, since it is probably the most well-known panfish in the U.S. There are numerous panfish species — bream, shellcracker, sunfish, yellow perch, crappie, rock bass, and so on — that exist in various areas of the country. But all of these panfish are so similar in size, life history, feeding characteristics, and fly preferences that I believe an understanding of a representative panfish, the bluegill, should allow you to improve your success on panfish, wherever you live and whatever panfish is most popular in your local waters.

Experienced fly fisherman and professional fishing writer that he is, I believe Dennis provides you in this book with a well-rounded, concise, and, most important, *user-friendly* summary of the life history and significant biological characteristics of the fish we like to fly fish for. In other words, this is not an academic treatise written by a fish biologist, *but a book written by a fly fisherman for fly fishermen*. Here you will find the information that will help you plan an intelligent strategy for every fish you will probably encounter in your fly-fishing life.

The book has two additional features which I hope you will find of value. After the description of each fish (or groups of fish with very similar feeding characteristics or fly preferences), I provide recommendations of the fly patterns that I have found to be most productive for me.

Second — and certainly a highlight of the book as far as I am concerned — you will see that the descriptions of the fish are accompanied by magnificent, full-color, anatomical illustrations by Montana's noted outdoor artist, Rod Walinchus. Dennis and I are both indebted to Rod for this fine contribution to our book.

For ease of reference, below each of Rod's anatomical illustrations, a page number reference to Dennis' written description of the fish is provided.

For more detailed information on some of the most popular species described in this guide, you might also want to consult these other companion volumes in the Library:

For brook, brown, cutthroat, and rainbow trout, *Fly Fishing for Trout, Volume I*, published 1992.

For Pacific salmon and steelhead, *The Teeny Technique for Steelhead & Salmon*, published 1994.

For largemouth, peacock, and smallmouth bass, *Fly Fishing for Bass*, published 1993.

For bonefish, permit, and tarpon, *Fly Fishing for Bonefish, Permit & Tarpon*, published 1992.

For amberjack, barracuda, bluefish, bonito, cobia, dolphin, grouper, jack crevalle, ladyfish, mackerel, marlin, mutton snapper, redfish, roosterfish, sailfish, shad, shark, snook, spotted seatrout, striped bass, tuna, wahoo, and weakfish, *Inshore and Offshore Saltwater Fly Fishing*, published 1995.

Bernard "Lefty" Kreh
Hunt Valley, Maryland

GLOSSARY

A number of specialized words have been developed by fish biologists to describe the anatomy and behavior of fish. If you are not already familiar with them, this short glossary, which includes a translation of the most often used scientific words into lay language, may be of assistance to you.

Anadromous — A fancy word for the habit some saltwater fish have of going to freshwater streams to spawn. A closely related — and even fancier — word is *amphidromous*, which describes fish that travel between fresh and saltwater, but not for spawning; snook and tarpon are amphidromous.

Anal fin — A single fin usually located just behind the fish's vent (or anus), unique because it's located in the middle of the fish's body, on the bottom behind the belly and in front of the tail. It's a stabilizing fin. Some species have spines on the front leading edge of the anal fin.

Billfish — A very informal term that is used by experienced fishermen for the various species of saltwater gamefish that have long pointed bills. Marlin, swordfish, and sailfish are all examples of billfish.

Dorsal Fin — A prominent fin located on the top of a fish's back. Most fish have two dorsal fins, referred to as the first and second. The first is forward of the second. On some species, the two are very similar, but on others they are different; fishermen often identify species by examining these dorsal fins. The different shapes and sizes of dorsal fins serve particular purposes for the various species of fish. So while to us the different fins may be interesting, to the fish they mean an easier life or a quick death.

Finlet — Lots of biological explanations, but the most useful meaning is "little fin." Finlets are usually located just before the tail, between the second dorsal fin and/or the anal fin. Again, for humans they are a means of identification; for the fish, a means of propulsion, stabilization, or sexual arousal.

Gill Plate — Sometimes called a gill cover. The hard surface that covers a fish's delicate gills so that nothing can come in from the side and damage them. The size and shape of a gill plate vary widely from species to species according to the function the gill plate serves. A gill plate can be light or dark, big or small, sharp (watch out!) or smooth.

IGFA — The International Game Fish Association, located in Pompano, Florida, publishes an annual report listing the world records for all gamefish species. There are several categories, including fresh and saltwater fly fishing and, more recently, catch-and-release. Call (305) 941-3474 for more information.

Kype — A strange word that describes the hook at the end of the lower jaw of male trout and salmon. It grows and becomes more pronounced during mating seasons. Some species have a kype on both the upper and lower jaws.

Lateral Line — All fish have this line, which is constructed of special cells running horizontally down the fish's sides. It's a sensory organ of remarkable capabilities. Many fish (snook, for example) also have a pigmentation variance right on top of the lateral line. For most fish, this pigmentation marks the lateral line. However, some lateral lines are camouflaged, and close examination is required to find them. Also, on a few fish species the pigmentation is above or below the lateral line.

Pectoral Fins — Two fins on the sides of the fish, up front behind the gill plates. Don't think of a human's pectoral muscles as an equivalent; on a fish, "pecs" are on the sides,

well forward. These fins are for locomotion and stabilization.
Pelvic Fins — Two fins on the bottom surface of the fish, on the forward part of the belly. The pectoral and pelvic fins are the same distance back on the body on many species. But many more fish feature one set of fins (usually the pectoral fins) slightly farther forward on the body than the other set.
Redd — A fish's "nest" in gravel or sand at the bottom of a river, lake, or pond. The word has been around a long, long time. It often gives novice fishermen away; if they don't know what a redd is, they're new to the sport.
Scute — (I had to look this one up.) "A horny, chitinous, or bony scale or plate." That definition's fine for biologists, but what about the occasional fisherman? Well, some saltwater species have these strange hard "bumps" on their sides, usually near the tail. On some species, they're between the second dorsal fin and tail, and/or the anal fin and tail. On a few species, the scutes run down the sides of the fish, near the lateral line. What occasional fishermen really need to know about scutes is that they can hurt. Be careful. Lastly, the placement, color, and number of scutes can help in identification.
Smolt — A confusing word. It generally means the young of many species of fish. But some species have different names for different phases of a fish's early life, so if you're not aware of all the names the locals have, you might use the word smolt inappropriately. It won't hurt the species — just your pride. If you're in doubt, say "baby fish" or "minnows."
Soft Rays — All fins on fish have rays, which are much like the veins of a leaf or the stem of a feather. Like these two examples, the soft rays in a fish's fins provide a framework for large surface area and little mass. For trees, this framework provides photosynthesis and shade. For birds, it provides lift, flight, and freedom. For fish, soft rays connect the thin material of a fin so the fish can move in the direction it wants to go. Hard rays are called spines.

Spine — A specially developed, sharp fin ray, usually just a few inches long. What's important to fishermen is how many each fish has and where they are. Most often, spines are found at the leading edge of one of the dorsal fins or at the leading edge of the anal fin. They'll stick you, and they hurt like mad. That's probably why the fish developed them in the first place — to deter predators.

Vermiculation — Another fancy word, meaning "worm-like." It's used to describe the coloration and pattern on the backs of some fish, such as the char and the brook trout.

OVERLEAF: *A brown trout. (See page 64 for description.)*

PART ONE

FRESHWATER SPECIES

AMERICAN GRAYLING
Thymallus arcticus

There's no mistaking the American (or Arctic) grayling for any other fish. It is famous for its dorsal fin, which is disproportionately large for the fish's size and arches back over the body in a beautiful display of color.

If you read about grayling in six different reference books, you'll unfortunately get six different versions of what the fish looks like. So let's just say that the fish is generally silvery with a few black spots on the sides, mostly on the forward half of the body. Except for the large, distinctive, spotted dorsal fin, all the fins are usually dark.

Some say the grayling looks like it's half Rocky Mountain whitefish and half trout, as accurate a description as any. To anyone accustomed to catching trout or whitefish, the grayling seems disturbingly familiar, with its whitefish body and its trout head and mouth.

But the grayling's overall coloration is what makes it so memorable. Where the fish lives, what it feeds on, and what type of light happens to be shining on the fish all have an effect on its appearance. Some say the fish is lavender, while others say it's green, and a few people see gold or bronze and silver. It's quite apparent from all this confusion that, like the salt-water bonefish, a grayling is mostly silver and therefore reflects the colors that are nearby. Diet, too, can affect the color of the flesh and scales.

My most unforgettable encounter with a grayling was in Montana's Madison River, just upstream from Ennis Reservoir. I was fishing for trout and had a good strike. As I reeled the fish in, I saw this huge dorsal fin sticking out of the water. It was fluorescent green! A pale fluorescent, yes, but certainly not grass green or blue green. It was brilliant. I brought the fish to hand, examined it quickly, and carefully let it go. I knew it was rare for those waters, and big — probably 1 1/2 or two pounds.

I've since learned that the male grows larger than the female. And while the male's dorsal fin is larger than that of the female, it is small and rounded in front and rises to a high peak toward the end of the fin. On the other hand, the dorsal fin of the female grayling starts out tall and tapers off. I'm guessing that single grayling I took from the Madison was a big female moving out of the reservoir and into the river in search of cooler waters.

Grayling never do get very large. All of the current IGFA records for grayling on a fly rod — most of which are only just over three pounds — come from Canada's Northwest Territories. Of course, history books will tell you of some tremendous lunker, but all of the IGFA fly-rod records were set in the 1980s, so the chances today of landing anything larger than three pounds are slim.

If you want to catch a U.S. grayling, you'll have to visit Alaska, Montana, Wyoming, Utah, or Idaho. Grayling are quite common in Alaska, but in the latter three states you'll need directions to find them. In Montana, there's a fair population in the upper stretches of the Big Hole River upstream from Wise River, but there are fewer each year. In Wyoming, most grayling are in Yellowstone National Park, and there are also some in the Green River drainage around Pinedale. A few other states have transplanted the fish, but the populations are extremely limited.

It is necessary to clearly distinguish the American grayling from the larger European grayling, which is often considered to be far more sporting than its American cousin. When many Europeans talk about fly fishing, they are talking about fishing for European grayling, as this is a highly esteemed fish in European waters, particularly those of the alpine regions of France, Germany, Austria, and Italy. The European grayling shares the same family as the American grayling, but it is an entirely different species. On the other hand, the two fish that are referred to as the Montana grayling and the (now extinct) Michigan grayling are probably subspecies of the American grayling.

Why anyone would fish for grayling with anything other than a fly is beyond me. With their small mouths and suspicious dispositions, they're *made* for fly fishing. Anglers in remote fishing camps in Alaska and northern Canada frequently catch so many grayling that they grow tired of them.

You should live so long. *(See p. 19 for color illustration.)*

Lefty's Fly Pattern Recommendations

The grayling has a tiny mouth and is basically an insect feeder. Since most northern insects are dark, flies such as the Adams, Royal Wulff, and dark Humpy, in patterns #16 to #12, are ideal. There are quite a few caddis flies in the grayling's habitat, so you'd do well to carry a few Elk-Hair Caddis patterns with you on your fishing trips. The fish strikes nymphs eagerly, so the Gold-Ribbed Hare's Ear, Zug Bug, and Dave's Squirrel-Tail Nymph are also productive patterns.

ARCTIC CHAR
Salvelinus alpinus

The Arctic char lives in cold water — as close to the North Pole as any freshwater fish gets. Its range includes all of northern Canada, Russia, Greenland, Iceland, Alaska, Norway, Sweden, England, Ireland, and Scotland. (Some even claim the char is found as far south as Maine and New Hampshire.) The fish living in the southernmost regions of these areas are usually the smaller, landlocked variety that only weigh two to eight pounds.

It's the northernmost anadromous Arctic char that really attracts sportsmen — fly fishermen catch record-sized char in the Northwest Territories, Labrador, and Quebec. The biggest char taken on a fly rod is listed at 18 pounds, although most Arctic char caught are less than two feet long and weigh under 10 pounds. Many a fly fisherman is trying to be the first to take a 20-pound char on a fly rod. The all-tackle world record char is 35 pounds.

The char belongs to the trout family, Salmonidae, whose many members share the same general body shape and a love for cool or cold clear water. From a fisherman's point of view, a char's closest relatives are the brook trout, Dolly Varden, bull trout, and lake trout, and since the char and these species may inhabit the same waters, identification can be difficult.

As a general rule, the Arctic char is olive green or blue on the back, occasionally also brown. Its sides are pale to bright orange or red, with few spots (if any) of cream or light pink. A spawner fresh from the sea is silver on its sides, with a little bluish black or green color to the back. The fish colors up considerably as it seeks out its home spawning waters, often in lakes or in slow-moving portions of rivers.

The landlocked char is routinely confused with the Dolly Varden and the brook trout. All three have pale spots on the

AMERICAN GRAYLING (15)

ARCTIC CHAR (18)

DOLLY VARDEN (40)

PINK SALMON (56)

sides and cream or white leading edges to all of their pectoral, pelvic, and anal fins. However, the char does not have the vermiculations of a brook trout on its back. And the char's spots are not nearly as colorful as those of the Dolly Varden and the brook trout; these two fish have brighter spots with circles around them.

But it is not difficult to tell an anadromous Arctic char from its cousins in early to late fall, when the char is in spawning colors. (Keep in mind that fall comes early near the North Pole.) A char in color is almost entirely crimson or bright orange — and we're not just talking about down the flanks. Many char turn bright red or orange all over.

Unfortunately, the operative word here is "many." Like the rest of the trout family, Arctic char can take on very different colors, even, to some degree, head and body shapes, depending on its environment. Available food, the distance the char is from the ocean, and water temperature and velocity can all change the appearance of a char returning to the ocean. An Arctic char from one continent may not closely resemble the char from somewhere else.

But when it comes right down to it, the only time you should really be concerned about the difference between a 10-pound Dolly Varden, a 10-pound brook trout, and a 10-pound Arctic char (which are huge sizes for these fish, by the way) is when you want to list the fish in the record books. Most fly fishermen would be real happy to have any of these fish of that size on their line. Their only goal is to have fun. Besides, when you're making a trip with the intention of catching a record-sized Arctic char, you should have a guide along. And if that guide can't distinguish between a very large char, a Dolly Varden, and a brook trout, you have a poor guide.

One more thing. If you're fishing for Arctic char, look around. You're standing in some beautiful country. Enjoy the view! *(See p. 19 for color illustration.)*

Lefty's Fly Pattern Recommendations

As mentioned above, the Arctic char ranges in size from one pound to more than 15 pounds. Hooks should correspond to the size of the fish: For smaller char, a #2 or #1 is fine, and for large char, you may want to use flies that are dressed on #1/0 or #2/0 hooks.

Brightly colored flies with a lot of flash are often best. A great pattern is a Clouser Minnow with a white underwing, a top wing of bright, fluorescent, salmon-pink bucktail, and a dozen strands of pink Crystal Flash in the middle of the wing. The same fly in white with green topping can also do well.

A favorite pattern of mine over the years has been a fly that I first saw in Alaska in the late 1960s and whose name I never discovered. However, I do remember it was constructed with a short tail of white marabou attached at the rear of the hook, with the body either unweighted, or weighted with lead fuse wire, depending on how deep you wanted to fish. A full "hula skirt" of silver Flashabou was added around the front of the hook, forming a collar that flowed back to the bend. This is a very simple pattern, and one I never fail to tie before going after char or Pacific salmon.

ATLANTIC SALMON
Salmo salar

The Atlantic salmon is the object of probably more wonder and awe than any other fish. This all began a long time ago.

The Romans became acquainted with the Atlantic salmon when they were pushing their way into Europe. The further north they went, the more villages they found dependent on the salmon for food. When they tasted it, the Romans became convinced that the locals were onto something. So historically, the Atlantic salmon was a table fish first, a gamefish second.

Descendants of some of these locals became downright protective of the Atlantic salmon, and for centuries, most of what was written about the fish was by British angler-authors. Immigrants arriving in America from Britain and the rest of Europe recognized the Atlantic salmon and called it "salmon" as they had back home. Unfortunately, some used that name for any fish that looked like a trout, including (when the immigrants got that far) the Pacific Coast rainbow trout and various species of Pacific salmon. Needless to say, this created some confusion for future generations of fishermen.

Early biologists named the Atlantic salmon *Salmo salar* because of its similarity to the brown trout, *Salmo trutta*. Due to the great confusion between the two fish, renaming the Atlantic salmon was seriously considered. However, it was decided that, given the fish's tradition (not to mention several hundred books written about this salmon), a name change would only make things worse.

To add to the confusion, young brown trout and young salmon (one to three-year-old parr, usually less than six inches long) inhabit the same waters and appear nearly identical. Each species is shaped like a trout, and each has parr marks (vertical broad stripes of gray or blue gray) and spots on its sides. However, a baby brown trout has halos around some of its spots and has more than two spots on its gill plates, while a baby Atlantic salmon has just two spots on its gill plates, and its tail is considerably more forked.

An adult Atlantic salmon returning from the northern Atlantic Ocean to its ancestral spawning stream (and incidentally, unlike Pacific salmon, the Atlantic salmon can spawn more than once) has a back color of blue, green, or black, bright silver sides, and a white belly. As the fish spends more and more time in freshwater, the sides darken, turning brown and bronze. A male picks up a little red on its sides as well and develops a kype.

Some say that an adult Atlantic salmon at this stage can be mistaken for a big, sea-run brown trout. And in some habitats that the Atlantic salmon and sea-run browns share (such as Norway and Sweden) this may be true, as sea-run browns in those watersheds can weigh as much as 30 pounds, the equal of most salmon. However, you should be able to distinguish a mature sea-run brown by its very square tail and its markings, which are dissimilar to those of the Atlantic salmon.

Historically, Atlantic salmon have reached weights that were astounding — up to 100 pounds. Today, the IGFA lists a 58-pound fish taken in Sweden in 1992 on 50-pound-test leader with conventional fishing gear. The three biggest fish listed in the fly-rod category weighed 47, 44, and 38 pounds. Of the salmon listed under the six fly-fishing headings, three were taken in Norway, three in Quebec. Most fly fishers will catch (and be quite happy with) Atlantic salmon weighing under 20 pounds.

Over the past 200 years, residents of the U.S. have read about Atlantic salmon fishing trips to eastern Canada, and now some acts of conservation have started to bring the Atlantic salmon back to streams in the U.S. Maine has a small transplanted population. The fish has also been reintroduced in the Connecticut River in the last two decades.

Many experienced Atlantic salmon fly fishermen estimate that it takes an average of 300 to 400 casts to achieve a hook-up on this magnificent gamefish. Atlantic salmon fishing is not a sport for the impatient.

For many anglers the Atlantic salmon remains the stuff of daydreams, but every year more fly fishermen are making their dreams come true. *(See p. 39 for color illustration.)*

Lefty's Fly Pattern Recommendations

Volumes upon volumes have been written about which flies to use when fishing for Atlantic salmon, and in the several hundred years that anglers have been tying for this fish, several thousand patterns have evolved. Still, there are a few that I think will do the job, providing the fly is drifted to the fish properly. Salmon flies are tied on a variety of hook sizes, depending on water conditions. On the Alta River in Norway, I have fished flies on #7/0 hooks, and I was told that bigger ones were often used. On smaller rivers, I have fished tiny, #10 low-water hooks with a fly pattern that would appear too small for fish the size of Atlantic salmon.

Here is a selection of flies I would carry on most salmon trips (all hair wings — I think traditional-pattern flies are fine, but hair-wing patterns are easier to tie and just as effective): Black Bear-Green Butt, Black Bear-Red Butt, Tippet Shrimp, Blue Charm, Thunder & Lightning, Rusty Rat, Bomber, and Green Machine.

BASS

Around the world, "bass" is a popular name for a number of species and subspecies of fresh and saltwater fish, such as the European sea bass *(Morone labrax),* its North American cousin, the striped bass *(Morone saxatilis)*, six species and four subspecies of the black bass *(Micropterus* spp.), and various tropical species.

But for most North American fly fishermen, there are really only two freshwater species that demand our attention. These are the largemouth bass and smallmouth bass. And as our travel horizons widen — more and more often the case these days — one freshwater species of the South American jungle can be added: the peacock bass. These three fish are discussed below.

The most popular species in North American saltwaters is the striped bass, which is discussed on page 139.

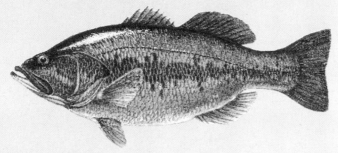

LARGEMOUTH BASS (26)

SMALLMOUTH BASS (28)

PEACOCK BASS (34)

LARGEMOUTH BASS
Micropterus salmoides

It's hard to give enough superlatives to the largemouth bass. Object of professional bass fishing tournaments, target of people of all ages for generations, "user friendly" to the point of developing nicknames like "bucket mouth" and "hawg." The largemouth bass is undoubtedly the best known of all the freshwater gamefish. Its popularity has made it a true economic force; there's money in largemouths, and lots of people know it.

The largemouth is the largest member of the North American sunfish family (Centrarchidae), which includes at least 30 known species. It is quite easily distinguished from the other five centrarchid species called black bass (Micropterus). The upper jaw of a largemouth reaches past the eye; this is not true of a smallmouth, another black bass.

The largemouth is much darker than the golden-hued smallmouth. A largemouth is burnt green with an unmistakable black, often wide, horizontal stripe that runs along the entire length of its flanks. On a large adult, the dark stripe can be hard to see when it blends in with the green.

This handsome fish is more ferocious than cunning or graceful. It is a relatively slow-moving fish and won't put up with moving water if it has anything to say about it — which it does — so it's almost always found in stillwater.

Its range initially extended from the waters of southeastern Canada, south into the Great Lakes, down into the warmer waters of the Mississippi River Valley, then on southward through the Deep South and into Mexico. In the eastern United States, the largemouth bass is also indigenous to the freshwater lakes and rivers from Maryland down the coast to the warm, rich waters of Florida. Today, the largemouth is one of the most adaptable and prolific bass in North America, and it lives in nearly all states of the U.S. Largemouth bass have been successfully introduced into freshwater throughout North and South America, including the colder waters of New England and some of the rivers of the Northwest.

Many experienced largemouth fishermen feel that Florida provides the best largemouth bass habitat anywhere. But some residents of our southwestern states challenge this, saying they just haven't been fishing for largemouth long enough in the Southwest to find out how large the fish can get there.

While the largemouth can survive in all sorts of water conditions, it favors warm, shallow lakes and rivers, the weedier or grassier the better. A heavy grassbed provides both cover and hunting grounds. It is uncommon to find significant concentrations of largemouths in deep water (below 15 to 20 feet) or in water without a lot of vegetation.

The largemouth spawns in water that has warmed to a constant 60 to 65 degrees F. In the southern reaches of its range, the largemouth will begin spawning as early as late April or early May, while farther north the water may not be warm enough for spawning until well into June or early July.

Largemouths are relatively long-lived. In northern waters, it is not uncommon for a largemouth to live more than eight years. And throughout this time, the fish keeps growing steadily, so that by its second full year as an adult, it will generally be between nine and 12 inches long. By the time it reaches full adulthood, say its eighth year, a northern largemouth may easily have grown to a length of 20 inches.

Because the water it prefers is rich with prey — worms, frogs, insects and insect larvae, minnows, and crayfish — and is warm nearly year-round, largemouths in the South generally grow at a much faster rate, especially in Florida. While a trophy-sized northern largemouth might tip the scale at eight pounds, occasionally Florida largemouth bass are landed weighing 12 pounds and more. In warm southern waters, bass anglers dream of 20-pounders. Some have been caught in Georgia, South Carolina, and California. *(See p. 25 for color illustration.)*

Lefty's Fly Pattern Recommendations

For many years the same old patterns were used for large-mouth bass, but during the past decade or so, a whole new set of flies has been developed.

Hook sizes for largemouth bass range from #4 for a smaller bass to #3/0 for a larger fish. The Dahlberg Diver is now an accepted killer on largemouths, fished as a popping bug or swum underwater. However, there is one fly, developed around the turn of the century, that has stood the test of time for both large and smallmouth bass, one that I would never be without — the Red and White Hackle Fly. I use it in lengths from 2 1/2 to seven inches, depending upon the size of the bass I'm after. A liberal dash of gold or copper Flashabou added to the pattern seems to increase strikes. Other flies that work very well on largemouths are the Clouser Minnow, Half & Half, Woolly Bugger, Lefty's Deceiver, Dave's Hare Jig, and various popping bugs.

All of these flies are explained in detail in a companion book in the Library, *Fly Fishing for Bass*.

SMALLMOUTH BASS
Micropterus dolomieui

I once heard Lefty Kreh say that if God declared that Lefty could fish for just one species of fish the rest of his days, he'd pick the smallmouth bass. He's not alone in his enthusiasm for the glorious bronzeback.

Many fishermen, including a great many who use flies, firmly believe that the smallmouth bass is the greatest freshwater fish living in the U.S. and Canada. It's a black bass with the instincts, fight, attraction, and class of a trout. Like its big cousin, the largemouth bass, the smallmouth belongs to the sunfish family and is one of six black bass species found in North American waters.

The bronzeback is a handsome bronze or brown and has dark stripes that run vertically down its flanks. The dorsal fin is continuous, only a small notch halfway back breaking the line. The mouth is relatively small, the upper jaw never reaching farther back along the body than the eye, but it is large enough to engulf good-sized minnows, frogs, and crayfish.

The smallmouth, like the largemouth, can be found throughout much of North America. Its range now extends from northeast Canada, south into Minnesota, then on into Maryland and Virginia, even as far south as northern Alabama. The fish is also found in some portions of the Midwest and into parts of Kansas and Oklahoma.

Originally, smallmouth bass in North America were confined to a fairly small area, mainly the drainage systems of Lake Ontario south through the Ohio River drainage. By the mid-1800s, however, smallmouth from the Ohio River were released into the upper Potomac, and by the middle of this century, they had been introduced into watersheds from Canada to California. For example, you can fish for smallmouth in the Snake River between Oregon and Idaho. Nevertheless, most of the great North American smallmouth water is in the East — principally, the Potomac, Shenandoah, Susquehanna, and James rivers, and their tributaries.

The smallmouth bass likes a stream or lake that is clear and flowing, and a rocky bottom with plenty of feed — smaller fish, insects, frogs, and crayfish. It does best in water that is cooler than the water preferred by the largemouth; the perfect temperature is between 67 and 71 degrees F. The warmer the water, the faster the smallmouth grows. A fish living in colder northern waters might need as many as three full years to reach seven to nine inches. But in warmer waters, it will probably reach the same length in two years or less.

Smallmouth spawn in lakes, mouths of streams, and in smaller tributaries. Active spawning begins when the water temperature rises and stays above 65 degrees F. In the southern limits of its range, rivers and lakes warm quickly and reach spawning temperature sometimes as early as April. Generally, by June or early July most smallmouth lakes and rivers have warmed enough for spawning.

The smallmouth bass can live as many years as a largemouth can, continuing to grow throughout its life — which now may be long, since a real catch-and-release ethic is being practiced by smallmouth fishermen. Obviously, a fish in water with better feed will grow larger than a fish whose feed is limited. A mature, seven-year-old smallmouth bass will generally measure between 16 and 20 inches long and weigh between three and five pounds.

The active fishing season for smallmouth bass begins in the spring in the southern regions of their range and lasts well into the fall. The smallmouth bass is usually most active during the early hours of the morning and later on in the final few hours of daylight. These are the times when the smallmouth actively feeds at the water's surface. This means, in turn, that when they're describing their smallmouth bass experiences, fly fishermen usually make references to early morning or sunset in their storytelling.

Those who have caught many species of fish on a fly rod say there's nothing quite like your first five-pound smallmouth on the light rod. Many make comparisons to trout, claiming the overall fighting characteristics are matched across the board. The skill and patience necessary to take a smallmouth with a fly are also compared to the skill and patience required in trout fishing and are held to be equally taxing.

Maybe Lefty knew what he was talking about. *(See p. 25 for color illustration.)*

Lefty's Fly Pattern Recommendations

As Dennis said, this is my favorite freshwater species in fly fishing. It's a tough fish to catch when it puts on a few pounds, and it fights very well. I love the environment it's in, too.

Just as anglers have developed many new patterns for the largemouth, so they have for this species. If you are after a smaller fish, then the little flies that have been around for years will work. Flies dressed on hooks #10 to #4 will take many smallmouths measuring six to 14 inches. But for a larger bass, the angler should consider a much larger fly; I often say that big smallmouth and largemouth bass want groceries. Fortunately, some dandy flies have been developed in the last decade for bass weighing two pounds or more.

The most effective big smallmouth fly I have used in the past half-dozen years has been the Clouser Minnow. I prefer it in four color combinations: white underwing and chartreuse upper wing; natural river shiner; baby bass; and baby walleye. If you are serious about catching larger smallmouth bass, I suggest you contact Bob Clouser, 1010 Ulrich St., Middletown, PA 17057, and obtain at least one of each of these patterns. Bob also makes an even larger fly for big bass, the Half & Half, a combination of the Clouser Minnow and the Lefty's Deceiver — a great fly. Another fly I recommend is the Woolly Bugger in all black, all chartreuse, or with a body of peacock, a black tail, and grizzly hackle.

The smallmouth bass probably prefers crayfish to all other foods, and the Clouser Crayfish is the best pattern I have used for it so far. In river current, just fish the fly on a dead-drift; in lakes, crawl it across the bottom after allowing it to sink.

OVERLEAF: *A gleaming redfish. (See page 124 for description.)*

PEACOCK BASS
Cichla orinocensis

I've had some personal experience with peacock bass in Venezuela and Colombia. To me, the whole sport is in the strike. The strike of a peacock bass is roughly what you'd get if you took a bowling ball and dropped it into a swimming pool from a three-meter board. The size of the hole in the water and the sound made by an aggressive peacock bass strike have to be seen and heard to be believed. Even then it's hard to register the speed and ferocity of a peacock.

A Venezuelan told me one day, "The last slow-moving fish in the jungle was eaten . . . 2,000 years ago!" He's probably right. All the critters in South American rivers are either on their way to eat something or are being eaten themselves. It makes for aggressive gamefish.

The peacock, a member of the freshwater Cichlidae family, is among the most interesting and colorful of the many bass-like species around the world. It looks a little like a largemouth bass with its big mouth and deep, massive body, but the resemblance stops there. If you were to use the predators that inhabit Africa's Serengeti Plain as an analogy, a speedy smallmouth bass would be the cheetah, the lurking largemouth bass the leopard, and the peacock bass, or *pavón* as the natives call it, would be the massive and magnificent lion. The male peacock carries the analogy even further; it has a big bulge on the back side of its head, somewhat reminiscent of a male lion's mane.

The peacock bass is now making a name for itself around Miami, where it is a relatively recent transplant. While no Florida peacock has ever grown as large as its South American ancestors, every year the fish is growing somewhat larger in the canals north and west of Miami and is developing a devoted following of fishermen. At the very least, the peacock bass is an alternative gamefish for this area. And at best ("in your dreams," as they say) it may someday weigh as much as 20 or 30 pounds!

The number of species and their common and scientific names are still open for debate. Some people recognize only two or three species, but others claim that when all the research is done, we may find there are as many as 12. For purposes of this guide, let's just stick with what little the author knows from personal experience.

In today's most celebrated peacock watershed, South America's Orinoco River basin, there exist three distinctive varieties of peacock bass: a big one with big stripes (usually three) down the sides; a little one with three dark circles down the sides; and another little one with what looks like dripping paint near the tail — distinct but indefinite streaks, stripes, or spots, like those of an appaloosa horse.

Indians on the Orinoco call the big peacock bass *pavón real,* royal or real peacock, for its size (huge) and for its eye spot, which is just in front of the tail. These peacocks can frequently weigh over 20 pounds, and record seekers swear up and down that there are 30-pound peacocks living in the Orinoco drainages. I believe them. *Pavón mariposa (mariposa* means "butterfly" in Spanish) is the local name for the small, three-circled fish. And the spotted guy is called *pinta de lapa,* after the name the locals use for a large, grass-eating animal that has spots on its rump, like . . . an appaloosa. The fish's common English name is spotted peacock.

The royal peacock's back is greenish black, its sides are yellow and orange, and its belly white or yellow. It has a large, black, ink-blotch marking on its gill plates, orangish fins on the bottom, and blue-green fins above. Textbooks say the eyes are red with a black pupil, but Indians have told me the eyes turn red during the struggle of being caught. They also claim that the butterfly peacock is simply a young royal peacock, and that, as it matures, the three circles of the young fish develop into the three bands of the larger royal. However, the *pinta de lapa* is thought to be a juvenile of another species altogether.

The fewer names the better, in my opinion, even if scientific research doesn't back up the Indians' theory. I think every fly fisherman should catch one 10-pound peacock bass somewhere in South America during his life. You owe it to yourself. *(See p. 25 for color illustration.)*

Lefty's Fly Pattern Recommendations

Most fly fishermen are not familiar with the peacock bass, but anyone who has caught one knows this is a superb fly-rod fish.

For surface presentations, the Dahlberg Diver is a favorite fly. Popping bugs will also take the fish. Underwater, bigger fish seem to prefer large flies, and the best fly I have tried is a large Lefty's Deceiver, at least six inches long. My favorite color combination is white with a topping of chartreuse and some silver or gold Flashabou on each side of the wing. The Half & Half is another fine peacock bass fly.

BLUEGILL
Lepomis macrochirus

Every fly fisher should know about the very popular American panfish, the bluegill, which has quite a few redeeming characteristics. For one thing, it's a glutton, eating just about anything, anytime. It lives in freshwater ponds, lakes, and reservoirs all across the country, and it breeds like a rabbit. The bluegill is one of the few fish species in which catching and keeping a limit is no problem. In most locales, there are enough fish to meet public demand, and in a few places, officials willingly let fishermen take more and more, just to keep down the populations.

General identification of a bluegill is not difficult. This member of the sunfish family (a big family) shares the same body shape as a cousin, the dollar sunfish, named for the old American silver dollar.

Besides its big, round body, the bluegill has a small mouth and head and a fairly broad, slightly forked tail. The body is compressed, so the fish is "thin" and "tall," sort of a pancake with fins. It uses its saucer-like shape very effectively when fighting against an angler's line. It's like fighting a living hubcap turned sideways in the water!

Coloration is not a key to identification. The bluegill may be dark or light or somewhere in between, according to where it lives, as water depth, temperature, and available feed apparently affect its coloration. The fish often lives among the weeds, which provide food and cover. Most bluegills will have about eight dark lines running down their sides, though these may be harder to see on some fish.

The gill plates on a bluegill have a marked, rounded extension that points toward the fish's tail. These "ears" (as some people who fish for bluegills often call them) are black or very dark blue, green, or brown.

To tell the bluegill from its many cousins, you can look for a black spot on the back half of its dorsal fin; elongated, tapered pectoral fins; and a mouth stretching no farther back than an imaginary line drawn down from the eye.

Even though the bluegill is referred to (erroneously) by a variety of names — rock bass, sunfish (several variations), pumpkinseed, warmouth, and redear — it is not any of these. But the blue sunfish, bream, and copperbelly *are* bluegills. Confused? Join the rest of the nation. Some fishermen in certain states have been calling our wide variety of panfish by the wrong names for generations.

The IGFA lists only *Lepomis macrochirus* in the pages of its record book, so if you're after a world record, look for the tapered pectoral fins and the black areas on the dorsal fin and gill plates. The biggest bluegill ever listed with IGFA weighed four pounds and 12 ounces and came out of Alabama in 1950. Current world fly-rod records range from one pound and eight ounces to two pounds and 12 ounces — all from Illinois, Colorado, North Carolina, and Oregon.

Bluegills never do get very big. In cold northern waters, a seven-year-old fish could well be only nine inches long. A 15-inch fish is about as big a bluegill as anyone can ever realistically hope to catch anywhere. Most bluegills taken are no larger than the palm of the person catching them. But these fish aren't caught for heft; they're caught for taste.

And finally, the greatest value of bluegills is that any fly fisher can get a beginner hooked on the sport by taking that person fishing for them. If you want to introduce someone you care about to fly fishing, drive as long as it takes to reach a bluegill pond. Your special companion will be sure to catch fish, and this will likely hook him or her on the sport you love so much. The two of you can then enjoy fishing forever, branching out to new fish species as you go. But you'll always have a soft spot for the bluegill.

Hail the lowly yet mighty bluegill! (*See p. 39 for color illustration.*)

Lefty's Fly Pattern Recommendations

Since the bluegill and its cousins in the panfish family are all small, they have small mouths. Flies are rarely dressed on hooks larger than #8; the most popular hooks for fly patterns range from #8 to #12.

When you are fishing any of these flies, it is important not to use a jerky or fast-moving retrieve. Bluegills and other panfish approach a fly with the intention of attacking it, but

ATLANTIC SALMON (21)

STEELHEAD (70)

BLUEGILL (36)

NORTHERN PIKE (43)

because of their small size, the fish are not sure that they can eat it or that it won't harm them. If the fly moves quickly or seems dangerous, panfish will avoid it. So very slow movements will produce the best results, whether the fly is underwater or on the surface.

Underwater flies generally produce best on bluegills and other panfish, which eagerly strike flies resembling nymphs, leeches, or other small underwater creatures. Any nymph used by trout fishermen is effective, as are small leech patterns, a Woolly Bugger, or a Sponge Spider (with rubber legs). One of the all-time best producers is a pattern with a body dressed with the thinnest chenille, wound at the front with a soft hackle (grouse or a similar fluffy, flexible feather). It's a good idea to tie this fly in sizes #8, #10, and #12, weighted with a few wraps of thin fuse wire, or unweighted. If I had to choose one pattern for bluegills, this would be the fly, in various colors and sizes, weighted or unweighted.

Bluegills and other panfish will readily take small popping bugs also. Poppers on #8 to #12 hooks and dressed with soft, flexible rubber bands are most effective. Most of the time, these mini-poppers should be worked slowly — never aggressively.

DOLLY VARDEN
Salvelinus malma

A lot has been written about the Dolly Varden, the colorful, anadromous gamefish of the Arctic and Rockies that inhabits the same waters as steelhead and Pacific salmon during certain times of the year. Unfortunately, a lot of the information out there is contradictory or confusing. In the paragraphs that follow, I've included only what several sources agreed on, avoiding scientifically obscure explanations and leaving murky issues alone.

First things first: the Dolly Varden is a char, not a trout. And it is colorful — its name comes from the red or pink spots on its side. The connection of red or pink spots and the name Dolly Varden takes a while to explain, but here goes: Charles Dickens wrote a novel called *Barnaby Rudge*. One of the characters was named Miss Dolly Varden, described as wearing a bright red mantle, or cloak. Several people in the Pacific Northwest have taken credit for naming the fish for the Dickens character between the years 1871 and 1881. While we may never know who was the first, at least we can be sure that in the 1880s "Dolly Varden" also meant a particular fabric featuring prominent pink spots that was used for dresses and curtains.

Other than these colorful identifying spots, some claim the Dolly also has light yellow spots on its dark, slightly vermiculated back. Others say there's a light blue halo around each spot on the side. Coastal residents are quick to point out that the Dolly, Arctic char, and several other anadromous fish are almost entirely silver when they first arrive in freshwater streams from the ocean, so any attempt at positive identification at that time is foolhardy. But in their prime, as the fish reach the head of their home waters, Dollys definitely have a pink or crimson shimmer to their sides, and their pink, red, and yellow hues are brilliant. A Dolly in full color is readily distinguishable from other members of the genus *Salvelinus* — the brook trout, Arctic char, lake trout, and bull trout.

Size is also another means of telling the difference between these species. A Dolly Varden rarely weighs over 10 pounds, quite often less. But the Arctic char and bull trout are generally much heavier. Some sources also indicate that a Dolly Varden's speckles are not as large as the fish's eyes, while an Arctic char's markings are bigger than its eyes.

The fish exists in virtually all the waters of Alaska and Arctic Russia. Landlocked Dollys do exist near the Rocky Mountains through Canada and the northern U.S., but they are so small that they are routinely mistaken for brook trout, juvenile lake trout, or bull trout. Only an experienced fisherman or guide can distinguish one of these small fish from another. Today, most American fly fishers will never see a Dolly Varden. Since its territory in the lower 48 states has shrunk so, the fish is a good deal more scarce at the close of the twentieth century than it was 100 years ago. The Dolly is still not well known. One thing is certain: anglers seeking big Dollys will be fishing in Alaska or Russia.

Many years ago, residents of Alaska paid a bounty for Dolly Varden tails, thinking the fish ate so many small salmon that they were a threat to the salmon fishery. Today's biologists admit that Dollys do indeed eat small salmon, but salmon and steelhead eat salmon and steelhead smolt as well. All in all, today's pundits claim, Dollys were unfairly misrepresented. If anything, Dollys are now generally more scarce than many salmon species.

The Dolly Varden is a very good gamefish that will indeed strike a fly. In prime condition, it's a good fighter, often amazing fishermen who come to isolated fish camps in search of steelhead or salmon. But in the fall there is little chance, in terms of color, of confusing a Dolly Varden with a steelhead or salmon.

Record seekers haven't paid much attention to the Dolly Varden so there are records to be had. This is just one reason to make the Dolly the designated fish of a planned trip, not just an afterthought. Another is the northern latitudes where these beautiful fish live. Nice country. Once in a lifetime stuff. *(See p. 19 for color illustration.)*

Lefty's Fly Pattern Recommendations
   As Dennis explains, a Dolly Varden is usually not large, although in Alaska, in a river mouth along the Bering Sea,

John Garry and I once found a huge school of Dollys where the average fish weighed 11 pounds!

The best hook size for a Dolly Varden is probably a #8 to a #1. The same patterns that work for the Pacific salmon also work for a Dolly. My favorites are a Woolly Bugger in fluorescent salmon pink, or a Clouser Minnow with a white underwing, a fluorescent salmon-pink upper wing, and some pink Crystal Flash in the wing. A pattern with a skirt of silver Flashabou (as I described in the discussion of the Arctic char on p. 18) is deadly on a Dolly.

NORTHERN PIKE
Esox lucius

You have to love pike to call them pretty. Shaped like a roll of Jimmy Dean sausage, the pike has a big, flat head, a large mouth with lots of teeth, and fins that appear to have been pushed to the back half of the fish. It's hard to call the northern pike beautiful and keep from smiling.

But those who know the pike love it. It is among the best-known of our freshwater fish, despite a range that extends from around the North Pole down to only latitude 60 degrees north. That means many U.S. fishermen looking for trophy-sized northerns, as they are often called, have to travel to Alaska or Canada to find them. Many, but not all.

The northern pike also lives in New England, in the Great Lakes states and as far west as Nebraska, and even eastern portions of the Dakotas. It is found throughout most of Canada, except in extreme eastern and western parts. Everywhere in between these coasts (including nearly all of Alaska) has been home to the northern pike since the Ice Age.

Pike-fishing stories are wonderful. Any gathering of fishermen soon generates a pike story, even if the fishermen are in the Bahamas on vacation. Stories abound of big fish hooked and being hit by even bigger fish. I saw this happen in northern Saskatchewan one summer. Textbooks claim a northern pike will strike anything that swims, including fish half its length. Many individual stories support this statement.

The pike family Esocidae is small: just three small pickerel species besides the northern pike and the muskellunge. I once asked musky expert Larry Dahlberg of Dahlberg Diver fame about the difference between a musky and a northern. His answer was succinct: "Musky are bigger and harder to catch." That about sums it up.

Fishermen new to the species can be sure they're catching northerns and not pickerel by the spotting pattern on the fish's sides. A northern has short yellow, light blue, or light green horizontal dashes on its dark green back and sides; the pickerel has dark splotches.

The northern pike is usually found in water three to five feet deep, rarely in water deeper than 15 feet, and usually in or near underwater plant cover. Its reputation for striking anything that swims by is well documented. One Canadian creel study ended up with so many different responses to its question about pike lures or bait used that it turned out to be practically useless.

While the northern pike will tolerate free-moving streams, it clearly prefers lakes, ponds, or reservoirs, where it is able to choose the water depth, temperature, or clarity. Scientific research has shown that the fish lives almost exclusively on minnows.

IGFA records for pike on a fly rod are in the 25-pound neighborhood; 40-pounders have been taken in Alaska and Europe by other methods. Catching a 20-pound northern pike out of a Canadian or Alaskan fishing lodge is not that unusual. Many pike fishermen land 10-pound trophies every summer — and that's not just in Alaska or Canada. Since the fish is a fast grower, any of its native range's ponds or lakes that are left alone for a year or two can provide some adrenaline-pumping surprises.

Some folks don't recognize the northern as a primary gamefish, considering it just a "back-up" for more celebrated species. But there are anglers who specialize in this fish. They spend time developing unique fly patterns, keeping records of lake temperatures, and so on. The northern pike, if not a gamefish, is definitely game. Ask anyone who's caught one. *(See p. 39 for color illustration.)*

Lefty's Fly Pattern Recommendations

The pike is the largest predator in its environment — and it fears nothing, not even a boat full of anglers. Because the fish often comes from behind, and opens its huge mouth to engulf the fly, you will need a long leader. I prefer about 30-pound-test braided wire that is at least 12 inches in length. For big pike (15 pounds or more) I like to use either a #3/0 or #4/0 hook, but for pike from three to 15 pounds, a #1/0 or #2/0 hook is adequate.

Three flies have given me great success. The Lefty's Deceiver in lengths of four to seven inches is my favorite fly, in red and white or all white. I often tie it with a weedguard when I'm fishing around lily-pad beds. Another is the Clouser Minnow, tied as long as you can make it with a white bucktail underwing, a top wing of chartreuse, and some gold or silver flash in the wings. Finally, don't neglect to try a leech pattern, since leeches are a primary food source for pike in some lakes. This is perhaps the easiest of all flies to tie. Place a hook in the vise, tie in a four to five-inch strip of black rabbit fur just behind the hook eye, and coat the wraps with epoxy. That's it!

One other fly I like to use when the pike are prowling the weed beds is a long streamer with a head made from Ethafoam, closed-cell foam that won't sink. Tie the streamer wing on the rear, construct a head like a Dahlberg Diver's at the front, and add a weedguard. This fly can be made very large and will cast easily on a 9-weight rod. The colors of the fly and head are unimportant.

PACIFIC SALMON

Unlike other well-celebrated anadromous fish such as Atlantic salmon and steelhead, all Pacific salmon share the fate of dying after their first spawning run from the ocean to their native freshwater spawning site. Six species of Pacific salmon are generally recognized by biologists, five of which species — the chinook, coho, chum, pink, and sockeye — have a native range from Taiwan to the entire Pacific seaboard of Alaska, British Columbia, and our western coastal states as far south as San Diego, California. A sixth Asian species, the cherry salmon, does not reach North American shores and is not included in this guide.

The chinook and coho have long been considered great sporting fish. But more and more these days, fly fishermen are discovering the value of chum, pink, and sockeye salmon as worthy angling opponents.

CHINOOK SALMON
Oncorhynchus tshawytscha

If you want to catch a chinook (or King) salmon in its native range, you'd better develop friends in Oregon, Washington, British Columbia, or Alaska. That's where the fish originated; the Great Lakes and New York populations as well as the more recent populations found in Chile and New Zealand's South Island are all the results of transplants. Fishing for chinook

CHINOOK SALMON (46)

CHUM SALMON (50)

COHO SALMON (54)

SOCKEYE SALMON (58)

with a fly is a unique experience, one that all fly fishermen should think of trying.

It's the size of the chinook — the biggest Pacific salmon — that attracts all the offshore sport fishermen in the Pacific Northwest. Thousands of chinook are caught each year from small boats bobbing in the rolling seas. But fly fishermen feel they have the edge in pure enjoyment, casting on coastal and inland spawning streams that comprise the chinook's migratory route.

Like all Pacific salmon, the chinook enters a freshwater stream looking the way it did in the ocean. A "fresh" or "bright" chinook is complete with sea lice, indicating it is newly arrived to freshwater and strong and feisty.

A bright King salmon is predominantly silver — white belly, silver sides, and darker back. There are dark spots on the back, down the sides to the lateral line, on the single dorsal fin, and all over the tail. These tail spots are unique to the chinook, so keep that in mind when you're trying to identify mature fish. Also look for dark color inside the mouth of a mature chinook and on the gums around the teeth, this color giving rise to one of the fish's many nicknames, "blackmouth salmon."

The chinook is a prime example of how nature assures species survival through overcompensation. There are chinook in many Pacific Northwest streams almost every month of the year. Why? Just in case. Volcanoes like Mount St. Helens may erupt, fire may destroy the headwaters of a small stream that is the spawning ground for two or three runs of chinook, drought may dehydrate and destroy miles of a small chinook stream. But nature provides against complete wipeout from natural disasters by providing a variety of time cycles for the chinook's spawning activity.

Today, however, the disasters brought about by humans are what are destroying the fish. Feeder streams to the Columbia River, for example, are now almost devoid of chinook salmon.

Chinook anglers learn just enough about all this to welcome the fish's presence in the waters they're fishing, appreciating the chance at a fish that can weigh from five to 80 pounds . . . on a fly!

In the IGFA record book, all six tippet categories have posted records, perhaps the most astounding being the 22-pound fish taken in New York's Salmon River in 1989 — on 2-pound-test leader! Three of the remaining records were taken in Alaska (29, 48, and 56 pounds), a 52-pounder came to a fly in Oregon's Chetco River in 1982, and the largest fish, at 63 pounds, was taken from the Trask River (which is also in Oregon) in 1987.

In a companion volume to this Library, *The Teeny Technique for Steelhead and Salmon,* Jim Teeny explains that Canadians have three names for chinook. Big chinook, those weighing up to 40 pounds or more, are called tyee or spring salmon. The smallest chinook, from two to eight pounds, are called jack salmon, and the chinook of sizes in between are called King salmon. But common names for fish tend to vary from place to place, so a King, for instance, might be called a tyee in some areas. Just be aware of the various names and ask if you're not sure.

You should also refer to Jim's book for detailed information on the tackle and fly patterns that Jim advocates for his Pacific salmon fly-fishing technique.

Most experienced chinook fishermen and biologists agree that the biggest chinook salmon usually arrive in freshwater streams in the spring. Keep in mind that spring in British Columbia or Alaska comes later than it does in Washington or Oregon. In the transplant streams in the Great Lakes and New York areas, chinook generally arrive in autumn. But over this large area, there is considerable variation, so it's best to consult local sources for the particular streams you're interested in. And if you don't already know the local timetables, you'll need to find some fishing friends in New York or around the Great Lakes before going after the king of salmon — the chinook. *(See p. 47 for color illustration.)*

Lefty's Fly Pattern Recommendations

Once they enter freshwater, the chinook, chum, coho, pink, and sockeye salmon all stop eating almost entirely, but they will occasionally eat the eggs of salmon who have spawned before them. The same flies work for all species, and most flies are tinged with bright fluorescent pink to imitate the eggs. These fish also occasionally feed on decaying flesh of dead salmon, so patterns such as the Ginger Bunny are effective.

Out of experience gained from 19 trips to Alaska, I recommend the following flies, which should handle almost all conditions there: Single Egg, Babine Special (sometimes called the Double Egg), Egg-Sucking Leech, Ginger Bunny, Purple Woolly Bugger, Olive Sculpin, and the unnamed fly constructed with the silver Flashabou skirt, described in my recommendations of patterns for the Arctic char (p. 18).

CHUM SALMON
Oncorhynchus keta

The chum (or dog) salmon is widely available in the waters of the Pacific Northwest and Alaska but has never been particularly popular with fly fishermen. Perhaps that's because in the lower 48 states the chum is a fall spawner, arriving as late as November or even December in many streams, after many anglers have quit fishing and settled in for the winter. In Alaska, however, chum begin to enter their spawning streams in July, and they are gaining popularity there.

A big chum weighs around 20 pounds; 30 and 40-pound record fish are by far the exception. But according to the IGFA record book, chum weighing 23 pounds have been taken on a fly rod in the 4, 6, and 8-pound-test tippet categories; in all three cases, that's a bigger fish than the record fish taken with the same pound-test leader with conventional gear. No other species can claim that achievement. The record fish were taken in Washington, Oregon, and British Columbia in the 1980s. Maybe it's time those records were challenged.

Except in Alaska, where chum retain their bright appearance for the first day or two after they enter freshwater, most chum salmon are unfortunately genetically programmed to start "breaking down" as soon as they hit freshwater, so they're tattered and generally beaten up by the time most fly fishermen see them. This unattractiveness doesn't help their lack of popularity, but their fighting ability isn't really affected. People catching chum salmon for the first time express surprise at how hard these fish fight. Chum have been known to take line and backing off a reel and pull them downstream behind themselves, and they have even broken quite a few rods, of all types and sizes.

A male chum has big, bared teeth on a kyped lower jaw. Some say that's why it got one of its popular nicknames, dog salmon. Others say it's because Eskimos feed chum salmon to their sled dogs during the winter.

Identifying a fresh or spawning chum salmon is not difficult, because it is the only Pacific salmon without black spots on its back. It does have black edges on all fins except the dorsal. In the ocean, a chum is primarily silver, and its back has a faint green tinge, occasionally accompanied by a very fine speckling of tiny black dots.

Once the chum hits freshwater (again, except in Alaska, where the fish will remain bright and beautiful for a few days) an amazing metamorphosis takes place in a very short time. The chum salmon after this change would fit right in at the camouflage department of a local hunting store. Both sexes look very similar; the female's colors are just somewhat more subdued. Vertical olive-green bars of different widths descend from its back at irregular intervals, most of the bars shaped sort of like a wood-block wedge — wider at the top and narrowing to points below the lateral line. These bars are matched by similarly shaped red bars that come up from the belly and extend well above the lateral line.

The belly of a spawning chum salmon is red, and the whole color display is overlaid with a patchwork of light and dark olive green. Some call it a "calico" look, but I think that's stretching the point to be nice. After its color change, a chum is a bad-looking dude. If it weren't a fighter, you probably wouldn't go after it.

Biologists say that most chum salmon don't tolerate freshwater too well and spawn relatively close to saltwater, within 100 miles of the ocean. There are some notable exceptions, however. In Canada's Mackenzie River, chum salmon are known to travel clear across the Northwest Territories to reach Alberta, some spawning in or near big lakes along the way, others continuing to the headwaters. Chum are also known to make similar long journeys in Alaska's Yukon River.

It's conceivable that the popularity of chum salmon will grow in the coming decades. Many fishermen are tired of crowded hot spots at popular times of the year. The chum salmon provide an alternative species and time of year that may seem more inviting as those decades overtake us.

But you don't have to wait that long. Make a few calls. Check it out. What are your late fall plans for *this* year? *(See p. 47 for color illustration.)*

Lefty's Fly Pattern Recommendations
  See Chinook Salmon.

A beautiful Atlantic salmon. (See page 21 for description.) ➤

COHO SALMON
Oncorhynchus kisutch

The coho salmon is often called a silver salmon because of its overall coloration. Once in freshwater on its spawning run, however, the coho's back darkens to a bluish black, and the sides lose some of their brilliance.

Coho salmon usually enter the ocean at the age of one year, and according to some studies, 90 percent return to their exact places of birth two or three years later. This could be due to the fact that most coho stay relatively close to the mouths of the rivers that brought them to the ocean.

Fly fishermen like the coho because of its willingness to take a fly, especially when the fish is fresh from the sea. While it's not as large as a chinook, the silver salmon is almost as popular, since it's so aggressive. Experienced fishermen say it jumps repeatedly and makes long, hard, fast runs.

The coho has a huge territory, one that stretches clear around the Pacific Rim. Since 1967, coho have also been found in Michigan and in other states surrounding the Great Lakes, where they were transplanted. But the Pacific Northwest is still the home of the biggest runs and boasts the longest tradition involving this salmon.

A big coho will weigh 20 pounds, and a few exceptional fish have been recorded at 30 pounds. Record fish taken on a fly rod listed in the IGFA book range from 15 to 21 pounds, all taken in Alaska. You may want to go there if you're looking for a record, but a lot of fishermen around the Great Lakes are perfectly content with what's close to home, as are many fly fishermen in Oregon, Washington, and British Columbia. There are still a few coho in the streams of Northern California, but darn few.

Coho start spawning in late summer and early fall, making them accessible at a comfortable time of the year for the angler. They're known to spawn well above the redds of sockeye, pink, and chum salmon, so they have some spawning redds to themselves. They also seem to like shallow, fast-moving water for spawning, and that too may help their breeding success.

At the end of the spawn, the females are just slightly darker than when they first entered the mouth of their natal river. The males have more pronounced changes, with both the upper and lower jaws extending and curving towards each other to such an extent that the fish can't close their mouths. They too get darker, and some develop a glint of red down their sides, like a rainbow trout.

To identify a coho, look at its spots and gums. The few spots a coho has on its back and sides are well above the lateral line, and only the top half of the tail fin has spots. A rainbow and a chinook have spots on both lobes of the tail. The gums of the coho are white, unlike those of the chinook.

When you scan the brochures put out by the fly-fishing lodges in Alaska and British Columbia, you'll see listed the weeks and months during which the various species of Pacific salmon are expected to be in the streams. The coho will always be prominently featured in this literature. The lodges' reasoning is that most fly fishermen can handle a coho, which is sized better and has a better disposition than the big, freight-train chinook that is so difficult to hook and land on a fly rod. If you run a fly-fishing lodge up north, schedule all your VIPs during the coho run. It pays to keep your important customers happy.

There's a lot of symbolism in those silver sides of a coho salmon. Maybe you should investigate. (See p. 47 for color illustration.)

Lefty's Fly Pattern Recommendations
See Chinook Salmon.

PINK SALMON
Oncorhynchus gorbuscha

The pink salmon shares basically the same watersheds as the other Pacific salmon species, but since the pink is the smallest member of the family, many fly fishermen do not consider it a particularly desirable trophy fish. Pink salmon caught on a fly rod and included in record books are listed as weighing 10 and 11 pounds, but, interestingly, those fish were taken on 2 and 4-pound tippets.

Biologists claim that while pink salmon make freshwater spawning runs from the Sacramento River in California clear around the Pacific Rim to Japan, the streams in British Columbia and Alaska have the largest, most predictable runs. "Large runs" in the case of pinks can actually mean bank-to-bank fish. Many a fisherman has returned from Alaska or British Columbia complaining there were so many pink salmon in the stream that finding enough open water to cast to other species was impossible.

The biologists' comments about predictability are also significant, because of all the Pacific salmon species, the "when, where, and how many" of pinks is the toughest to predict. Textbooks tell us they spawn every other year, but there are at least two strains for every watershed, and every fall there are at least some pinks in the stream as early as July, maybe as late as November. Add the fact that one year's run is definitely larger than the other and usually composed of significantly larger fish, and you have enough variables to make any prediction suspect. On top of all this, many pink salmon don't bother returning to their natal stream, going elsewhere instead. What it comes down to, then, is that there may or may not be pink salmon in the Alaska or British Columbia stream of your choice, but there is a good chance they'll be there if you're at the stream in late summer or early fall.

Pinks spawn in coastal estuaries or in freshwater just a few miles in from the ocean. But, as with the other species of Pacific salmon, there are always a few notable exceptions. In Alaska and British Columbia, pinks have been known to travel hundreds of miles inland.

In saltwater, the pink salmon is generally silver all over. High on its back there are big black spots, and large, oval-shaped black spots distributed evenly on both lobes of the tail. These spots are important for identification. A mature male pink salmon has a huge humped back, from which it gets its most enduring nickname, "humpy." The male also develops a distinct pink down its sides during spawning and develops a kype on both the upper and lower jaws.

It's not the color of its skin, however, that gives the fish its name, but rather the pink color of its flesh. All other salmon have red or white meat. Some say the lack of red color in a pink's flesh means lack of oil, making the flesh less tasty. Others claim less oil means lower cholesterol. So, for some, the pink is today's preferred eating fish. Go figure.

Let's address the pink's small size and low esteem with anglers. I was fishing for steelhead in the Dean River in British Columbia. It was August and the watershed was suffering from a drought, but very recent rains had made the river high and so murky that you couldn't see a fly in eight inches of water. In short, fishing was lousy.

But the pinks were in. Not in large numbers, but enough to give you something to cast for. Using 6-weight fly rods with 6-pound-test tippets, we caught a few fish every day. The pinks hadn't read any of the biologists' reports and neither had we. The fish and fishermen met on a neutral playing field and had a contest. It was great sport. If the pinks had not been around, there would have been no game at all.

I submit (again) that sport is where you find it and that, in the future, enterprising young men and women are going to figure out ways to make fishing for pink salmon with a fly rod a tremendous, "new" sport.

I hope so. I hate crowded streams. *(See p. 19 for color illustration.)*

Lefty's Fly Pattern Recommendations
See Chinook Salmon.

SOCKEYE SALMON
Oncorhynchus nerka

If you've ever had salmon from a can or enjoyed grilled salmon at a restaurant or backyard barbecue, chances are you were eating sockeye (or red) salmon. The flesh of the sockeye is very red, full of oil and therefore tasty — some say delicious. Not all commercial salmon is sockeye, but they're the most sought after and bring the highest price.

As a gamefish, the sockeye receives mixed reviews. Some visitors to Alaska, where the fish is most accessible in large numbers, say there is no sport to it; too many fish, no means of properly presenting a fly. In *The Teeny Technique for Steelhead and Salmon*, Jim Teeny disagrees, saying he loves fishing for sockeye with a fly rod. Considering the many years he's been developing flies for steelhead and salmon, and the countless streams he's fished, I'll side with Jim Teeny. I suggest you take a look at his book to learn the technique he advocates to properly present and retrieve the fly to a sockeye.

The sockeye ranges farther north than other Pacific salmon. The Klamath River in Northern California is as far south as it gets, and it's found in coastal rivers clear around the Pacific Rim to Japan.

But most sport fishing for the sockeye is done in Alaska, which is where all the fly-rod records come from. Most of these record fish weigh about 11 or 12 pounds, and, interestingly enough, those taken by other types of tackle are not much larger. The usual sockeye caught weighs between four and nine pounds.

Like all Pacific salmon, the sockeye is silver in the ocean, where it can be distinguished by the lack of large spots on its back or body. Once in freshwater, a male sockeye turns a brilliant red; hundreds of these fish together make the bottom of a small stream appear red and *moving!* The female is also reddish, but this color is muted by olive green, and the fish's sides are somewhat darker.

Sockeye will spawn in streams but much prefer lakes. They'll spawn in gravel rather than rocks, and their redds are very close together. Thousands of pairs of sockeye will occupy a relatively condensed area. It's great for nature watching but can be calamitous when a disaster strikes or humans intervene in their life cycle. A lake on the highest headwaters of the Salmon River in Idaho called Redfish Lake was named for the sockeye that used to nearly fill it each fall. Sadly, sockeye can no longer run the 900 miles (past eight dams) to make the name Redfish Lake have any meaning.

But in Alaska, especially in the Bristol Bay area, sockeye are still migrating by the millions. The young live in an inland lake or stream for up to three years, and two to six years in the ocean.

A few words need to be said about the landlocked sockeye, called kokanee. They occur naturally everywhere throughout the sockeye range. Kokanee are also fall spawners, often running upstream out of lakes of reservoirs into feeder streams. Although smaller than their ocean-going cousins, kokanee provide good sport and eating to thousands of anglers around the world. Japanese and Russian fishermen know about sockeye and kokanee. Fishermen in all the Pacific Northwest states and provinces do, too.

If an angler had his druthers, he'd just as soon fish for sockeye, chinook, or coho. But if there are kokanee available in his own back yard, it's easy for him to become content with what's at hand.

As a brief summary, sockeye salmon are brilliant red, better sport when they're fresh or bright and, although available throughout the Pacific Northwest, are most plentiful in Alaska. And according to Jim Teeny, Lefty Kreh, and others, a strong fighting, worthy opponent on a fly rod. *(See p. 47 for color illustration.)*

Lefty's Fly Pattern Recommendations
See Chinook Salmon.

TROUT

There are four major species of trout most commonly sought after by modern American fly fishermen — brook, brown, cutthroat, and rainbow (and its anadromous kissing cousin, the steelhead). These species vary in many ways: in size, lifespan, feeding habits, spawning behavior, temperature tolerances, environmental requirements, and so on. These variations are critical to an understanding of each species and how to fly fish for them successfully.

BROOK TROUT
Salvelinus fontinalis

Many older trout fishermen remember the brook trout as the first fish they ever caught. In his 1972 book, *Trout Fishing*, Joe Brooks talks about his experience with a brook trout as a boy. He took the six-inch trophy home and had it for break-

BROOK TROUT (60)

BROWN TROUT (64)

CUTTHROAT TROUT (66)

RAINBOW TROUT (68)

fast the next morning, claiming it was the best fish he had ever eaten. Ernest Schweibert devoted more pages to the brook trout in his two-volume book, *Trout,* than any beginning fly fisher would think possible. His chapter on the species is entitled "The Aphrodite of the Hemlocks." You'd have to have gone fishing for brookies in Michigan or Maine to fully appreciate this title.

Brook trout have been described by many writers as "jewels." They are beautiful. The back is dark green, with dark gray or black vermiculations that continue over the top part of the tail. The tail is squared off, accounting for the fish's most popular nickname, "square-tail." The upper side of a brookie also has vermiculations, as well as a great many light green oval spots. Most impressive are the few red spots surrounded by blue halos on the sides of the brookie. This combination of spots and halos helps distinguish the brookie from a bull trout or Dolly Varden.

The sides of a male brook trout in full fall spawning colors are brilliant orange. The fins of the lower body, which are orange the rest of the year, take on a little more red, and the white edges of the front of all those fins seem brighter. The normally white belly appears to have picked up a dusting of copy-machine toner.

Brook trout are indigenous to the area extending from Michigan to Maine, down to Georgia, and back up into Canada, but today their numbers are badly depleted. Early in the nineteenth century brookies were exported west, taking hold only in the streams that remained clear, unpolluted, and well below 70 degrees F. all year long — that is, in the high country of the Rocky Mountains.

In many western states, fishing regulations involving the brook trout are still quite lenient. However, with the number of brookies living in beaver ponds, high-altitude lakes, and big lakes and reservoirs, there is little danger of depleting the supply. And in Argentina, New Zealand, and some lakes in the Rockies, five to 10-pound brook trout are not rare. IGFA record brook trout taken with a fly rod come from Canada, all ranging in weight from eight to 10 pounds. Many well-traveled fly fishers are convinced that 15-pound brookies are out there somewhere.

But for most trout fishermen, memories of brook trout involve small fish. I remember fishing for small brook trout by myself on the Big Lost River in central Idaho when I was less than 10 years old. My father was smart enough to know that if he left me by a beaver pond with 20 to 40 brook trout in it, I'd stay there. And he was right! I can still remember crouching over clear water, watching brookies move to my worm, jerking them out, wrapping them in grass, and saving them for my Great Uncle Hoot, owner of the farm where we fished. He would accept only scaleless brook trout as payment. I gave him all I caught — none were over 12 inches long, most under 10. He liked to fry the fish in bacon grease until the skins were crisp just like bacon. I guess my Uncle Hoot and Joe Brooks had something in common. (*See p. 61 for color illustration.*)

Lefty's Fly Pattern Recommendations

The brook trout could well be considered the most beautiful of all trout species. It is usually not as wary as the other trout and tends to accept flies more readily. Brook trout that live in smaller streams will take just about any well-drifted dry fly as well as nymphs.

Larger brookies will accept dry flies during hatches, but the best patterns to use are streamers, particularly gaudy streamers. The Mickey Finn has been responsible for more strikes from brookies than any other fly. Streamers with red, white, or yellow in them are effective, as are Woolly Buggers constructed in dark colors.

BROWN TROUT
Salmo trutta

Brown trout are Europe's native trout but were introduced to the U.S. from German and British stocks in the late 1880s. Cynics have said the brown trout was established everywhere the British army went, because the officers insisted on fishing for browns for sport. True or not, the statement can't be far off, because today brown trout are seemingly everywhere. Lodges in New Zealand, Argentina, Arkansas, Utah, Montana, and New York today make a living off their reputations for big brown trout. The fish gets around.

Many people talk about how smart a brown trout is, although its brain is smaller than a pea, like any other trout's. But since European anglers have been fishing several hundred years longer for the brown trout than we have for our native trout species, the brown has apparently developed stronger survival instincts, which often — but not always — make it harder to catch. And it can survive in waters that other trout can't tolerate. It has managed to survive in Europe's badly polluted waters for a long time.

A brown trout is mostly brown or yellow brown, with black dots from its sides upwards, including the upper portion of the tail. On most mature fish the tail is square at the end. Some red or bright orange dots are usually scattered down the sides, and these markings tend to be encircled in light blue.

As they became more and more solidly established in American rivers and reservoirs, brown trout began to develop regional color patterns. A brown trout from the Missouri River in Montana does not look exactly like a brown trout from a Pennsylvania limestone stream. Many fly fishermen take photos of the fish they catch before they release them, and over the years, pictures of different brown trout from different areas demonstrate the similarities and the differences.

At last count, brown trout were living in 38 of the lower 48 states. Most states can boast that anglers catch 10-pound, even 20-pound fish in their watersheds. IGFA records on a fly rod show 10 and 12-pound fish taken in New Zealand on 2 and 4-pound tippets; 27 and 29-pounders taken in Argentina on 12 and 16-pound-test tippets; and a 27-pounder taken from Utah's Flaming Gorge Reservoir on an 8-pound tippet.

Technically, the brown trout is closer to the Atlantic salmon than to other trout species (note the genus names), but in the minds of fly fishermen, brown trout mean streamers, nymphs, and dry flies, sometimes minuscule. And it makes little difference whether you're dredging streamers in Arkansas' White River or skating #22s on the Big Hole in Montana. The expectation is the same: a hard hit and a good fight. (See p. 61 for color illustration.)

Lefty's Fly Pattern Recommendations

If you are looking for a fish that's tough to fool in freshwater, the brown trout fits the bill. Brown trout may be as short as six inches or as heavy as 25 pounds, so fly patterns have to be chosen according to the size of the fish you expect to take. If you're using a dry fly, it's best to match your imitation to the type of flies that are hatching. If there are big drakes about, use a large drake pattern. If small emergers are coming to the surface, you should use a small emerger imitation or a Griffith's Gnat. A very large brown trout will often feed on very tiny flies when the flies are hatching in great numbers. Nymphs are always a good bet.

But for the largest brown trout, streamers are best. Sculpin flies perform better when they are fished along the bottom early and late in the day; they are usually not as effective during the middle part of the day because sculpins are nocturnal. Zonkers, Woolly Buggers, Matukas, Clouser Minnows, and even Lefty's Deceivers are all effective patterns. Since brown trout feed at night more than any other trout, bulky or heavily hackled dark flies are best at that time because they "push" water as they move, creating sound waves which allow the trout to locate them in total darkness.

CUTTHROAT TROUT
Oncorhynchus clarki

I'm not even going to pretend to be objective here; the cutthroat trout is "my" fish, the one I love above all others. It was food for animals and indigenous people for thousands of years before European settlers traveled west. This trout is a part of the past.

The cutthroat is the native trout species in 10 of the 11 western states. The current expert on the cutthroat, Robert Behnke of Colorado State University, believes there are four major and 10 minor species; many of the western states have their own unique cutthroat subspecies.

One of these types is the Lahontan cutthroat, which grows to over 10 pounds in Pyramid Lake north of Reno, and fills all of the IGFA record categories for cutthroat. But the IGFA only recognizes one general species of cutthroat, *Oncorhynchus clarki*. The Lahontan, now called *Oncorhynchus clarki henshawi*, is a largely bluish and silver lake fish with few spots. It looks like an anadromous coastal cutthroat that is fresh from the sea. Coastal cutts have the dubious distinction of being referred to as *Oncorhynchus clarki clarki* by scientists and range from Northern California to Alaska, often as far as 100 miles inland. Cutts with fair-sized populations in isolated locations include the Yellowstone, West Slope, and Finespotted Snake River cutthroats. The Paiute, Humboldt, Bonneville, and Whitehorse cutthroats are also localized, but their numbers are dwindling.

A cutthroat has a red or orange slash line on the underside of its lower jaw, hence the name. Most species and subspecies feature black spots on the back and sides, a tinge of red or pink on the sides, and orange or yellow pectoral and anal fins. With 14 different types of this fish, there are exceptions to almost every general description of the cutthroat, so study the regulations and pictures carefully if you've never fished for cutthroat before.

Westerners call the cutthroat a "native" and claim it doesn't fight as well as a rainbow or a brown trout. That's true enough, but it does rise exceptionally well to dry flies and can be very picky in areas where it is heavily fished. A friend from New York, Paul McKenzie, once told me in Idaho, "I've just had 32 refusals in this one hole!"

Unfortunately, over the course of the last 150 years, we've practically eliminated some of the cutthroat species and subspecies. Populations are hanging on to existence by mere threads. Brown trout and rainbows inhabit most major streams in the West, streams the cutthroats originally had all to themselves. I just hope there will be enough cutthroat around to last my lifetime.

And if in heaven there are no streams and no cutthroat trout, I'm not staying. Heaven would be a different cutthroat species every day that was a little bit hungry and had never seen an artificial fly.

Heaven without cutts? I can't imagine it without them. *(See p. 61 for color illustration.)*

Lefty's Fly Pattern Recommendations

The cutthroat is almost as easy to fool as the brook trout. It appears to be unaware that the fisherman is its enemy, and, consequently, almost any well-placed dry fly or nymph — often even a streamer — will catch the fish. A whole host of fly patterns will do the trick.

RAINBOW TROUT
Oncorhynchus mykiss

The rainbow is probably the best known of all trout; it's what most people think of when the word "trout" is spoken. They envision a brilliant red stripe down the side of a silver fish, and black spots down the back, over the dorsal fin, and down through the tail. And if they're lucky, they remember a big, white mouth sucking in a dry fly.

Rainbows are popular too because they fight well. Or, to be more specific, they leap out of the water in high arches that thrill the most hardened souls. It's a grim man or woman who doesn't get a thrill out of seeing a rainbow jump at the end of his or her line. Rainbows are spectacular fighters, and many people fish for them, exclusively, for that one reason alone.

It's also popular because of accessibility. The rainbow was originally native to just the west coast of North America, from California to Alaska, but it now lives in cold-water watersheds in every U.S. state and on most of the continents and islands of the world. Rainbows survive. Managers of fish hatcheries have fewer problems with the rainbow than with any other trout, and rainbows will live in areas where the cutthroat and brook trout die out; and if the water temperature is cool enough, even in waters that the brown trout can't hack.

Any experienced trout fisherman can tell stories of rainbows muscling other fish out of a pool. They're aggressive. The West Coast was no picnic, even 300 years ago, and rainbows developed good survival instincts.

In addition to the rainbow species, *Oncorhynchus mykiss*, there are five subspecies listed in the most recent scientific monographs. The most common subspecies is *Oncorhynchus mykiss irideus*, the coastal rainbow that is at once the steelhead and the rainbow. The other three subspecies come from three rivers in Northern California and are better known to trout fishermen by their river names than by their Latin names. There's the Fraser River rainbow *(Oncorhynchus mykiss gairdneri)*, two from the Kern River *(Oncorhynchus mykiss aguabonita* and *Oncorhynchus mykiss gilberti)*, and the McCloud River rainbow *(Oncorhynchus mykiss stonei)*. All rainbow come from one of these original strains.

Most rainbow trout have a red or pink color on their gill plates, marking the beginning of the red flank stripe. Many fish have reddish or pinkish fins on the bottom sides of their bodies, but not all. Some rainbows have lived in a lake, reservoir, or stream so long they have developed different colorations from their ancestors, becoming very silvery, for example. But the shape of the tail has always stayed the same — not very notched, not square either, with spots all over.

It would be impossible to calculate the number of hours of enjoyment that the rainbow trout has given fly fishermen all over the world. If you have never fished for a rainbow with a fly rod, you're in the minority of folks reading this book.

You will note that in this guide I've treated the exclusively freshwater rainbow and the anadromous steelhead as different species of fish. I know in my mind that's not so, but not in my heart. The scientists tell us they are the same fish, but I'll bet these scientists aren't anglers. Saying a rainbow is the same as steelhead is like saying a purebred racehorse is the same as a big workhorse. They may have the same DNA structure, but they look different and perform differently. I fish steelhead for one reason, rainbows for another. So does everyone I know. Come on, biologists — can't we at least change the subspecies name? For crying out loud. *(See p. 61 for color illustration.)*

Lefty's Fly Pattern Recommendations

The rainbow won't accept your offering as recklessly as the brookie will, but, on the other hand, it is usually not as wily as the brown trout. It often prefers faster water, and that sometimes calls for slightly different patterns. When the runs are fast and the water is choppy, dry flies that float well are needed. Parachute flies do well, as do the Humpy and the Trude. When rainbows are very cautious, you'll need to match the hatch. Few rainbows can resist a well-presented nymph that imitates the nymphs they like to feed on.

STEELHEAD
Oncorhynchus mykiss irideus

The steelhead is the stuff of legends. In this decade, there may have been more magazine articles and books written about this species than about the other featured star of angling literature, the Atlantic salmon. That's saying something.

The range of this anadromous rainbow trout was initially restricted to the Pacific Northwest, but its territory has since expanded. There are now steelhead in Idaho, the Great Lakes, upstate New York, Russia, and Japan. A Colombian angler told me there was even a steelhead run in his country. When I asked him how that was possible, he explained that since the Andes in Colombia are very close to the Pacific, snowmelt keeps certain streams cold all year long, providing ideal steelhead habitat. This may or may not be true, but it's plausible.

There's some confusion out there about the Latin names for the steelhead and the coastal rainbow trout, which is a subspecies of the rainbow. For a long time, biologists insisted the two were the same fish, calling them both *Salmo gairdneri irideus*. Now we're being told we should call them *Oncorhynchus mykiss irideus*. This change doesn't seem to affect the fish or fishermen too much.

If you know the steelhead, you don't need a physical description. If you've never seen or fished for steelhead and are reading about them for the first time, my job is a tough one. A description of steelhead depends on where you are.

Steelhead spawn in rivers from California to Alaska (also in the Great Lakes and New York), and some rivers have four runs a year, most rivers just one or two. The steelhead's appearance varies according to the river, the time of year, the available food in the watershed, and other variables. Some fish are exceptionally silver, others are very dark, still others are green and red or steel blue and silver.

As a general rule, a steelhead looks like a big rainbow trout, which it is; but this statement will make some steelheaders cringe. Sure, the steelhead and rainbow have the same big, red band down the side, the same white mouth, and the same little black spots all over the back, sides, and tail. But a fresh steelhead in most Pacific Coast streams is almost entirely silver — so hard to see that spotting the fish becomes a big part of the sport.

In its spawning waters, a steelhead turns dark, the male becoming darker than the female. In the Salmon River in Idaho, I once caught a native, wild-strain male steelhead that was so green and red it looked like a Christmas-tree ornament. From the same river, my cousin took a bigger fish that was silver and blue and had nearly no spots.

Fishermen in Alaska, British Columbia, Washington, Oregon, California, Idaho, New York, and the Great Lakes all have favorite local streams for steelhead and know when to fish for them. Now we're discovering that the Russians (and the Yankees visiting them) are developing their own seasonal calendars for chasing steelhead. For many anglers, going fishing for steelhead is just half a step short of going on a holy pilgrimage. I know people who have quit full-time jobs so they could go after this fish.

If you belong to that unfortunate group that knows nothing about steelhead, don't lose any more time. There are scores of books and magazines out there that can tell you all you need to know very quickly. When you catch your first steelhead, you'll remember it forever. The fish will probably weigh less than 10 pounds, but you'll have heard of 20 or 30-pound steelhead, and you'll go back again and again and again and again. *(See p. 39 for color illustration.)*

Lefty's Fly Pattern Recommendations

The steelhead and Atlantic salmon are certainly the most energetic, acrobatic fish in freshwater. Both return to their natal rivers to spawn and tend to hold at very specific locations in pools year after year.

When fishing wet flies for steelhead, once you've located a fish, you need to drift the *underwater* fly without drag to the fish *at the level in the water column where the fish is holding.* This is more important than the type or color of fly pattern used. If the fly is too far above or below the fish, the steelhead will rarely strike. Most steelhead flies carry little weight, so experienced anglers use various sinking fly lines that will sink at different rates.

There are numerous effective underwater fly patterns, many incorporating fluorescent or bright colors. Some have Cactus Chenille or another bright, flashy Mylar material to attract the fish. Others, such as the Comet fly, have weighted, bead-chain eyes that drive the fly deeper in faster water. For decades Jim Teeny has used nothing but his Teeny flies.

Dry flies for steelheads can also be effective. The standard technique is to dress the fly with a floatant that is usually greasy, such as silicone, and cast it across and downstream so that the line and leader drag the fly across the surface, forming a wake behind it. I prefer, instead, to grease most of my leader to make the fly skitter better on top of the water. The strike of the steelhead on a dry fly that (hopefully) follows is the most difficult strike to master in fly fishing. The fish opens its mouth and sucks in the fly, so if you strike immediately, as you normally would, you have a good chance of missing the fish. You need to allow enough time for the fly to go deep in the steelhead's mouth and then for its mouth to close. When the fish breaks the surface to accept the fly, *drop the rod tip in the direction of the fish* so the fly can fall deeper into the mouth. Then strike.

OVERLEAF: *A sailfish breaks the surface of the water. (See page 89 for description.)*

PART TWO

SALTWATER SPECIES

AMERICAN SHAD
Alosa sapidissima

The most vivid memories of fly fishing for shad are of time and place: spring in coastal rivers heavy with runoff. Since shad are anadromous, fly fishermen on the Atlantic and Pacific Coasts routinely take advantage of the spring spawning runs to break the doldrums of winter. For many, the shad run is the first time each year that they can pick up a fly rod. Something that significant you remember.

The American or white shad, *Alosa sapidissima,* belongs to the herring family. It has the compressed body, the thin scales, and the curved belly of the oceanbound skipjack herring, without its weak teeth or the sharp-edged scutes on its belly. The American shad's lower jaw does not protrude like that of the skipjack herring and of the white shad's nearest American relative, the hickory shad. Instead, when the American shad closes its mouth, the upper jaw engulfs the lower. Of the six species of the *Alosa* genus, the American shad is the largest, attaining a length of two feet or more and generally weighing between 1 1/2 and eight pounds, even occasionally as much as 10 or 12 pounds.

A Rocky Mountain trout fisherman would say the white shad looks something like the Rocky Mountain whitefish, and a saltwater angler would compare its shiny appearance to that of a bonefish. The adult American shad has a row of black spots behind its gill plates. The predominantly silver body has a single dorsal fin on top of the middle of the back. The upper rows of scales have well-defined dark lines which form faint lines on the sides of the adult.

The amazing thing about shad is their vast territory along both coasts of the United States. On the Atlantic side, American shad spawn in major coastal rivers all the way from Florida to Canada's Gulf of St. Lawrence. They're widespread in Connecticut and Massachusetts, throughout the Chesapeake drainage system in Maryland, and in the Carolinas, Georgia, and Florida. Their location changes with the seasons.

Shad first start appearing in November and December in the warmer waters of Florida's rivers, spawning as far south as the St. Johns River. The schools gradually work their way up the coastline, the run peaking in the Connecticut River in May and the Gulf of St. Lawrence the next month. Sadly, the runs are down so badly in some East Coast states that shad have been placed on the endangered species list. So it's wise to check local regulations before you fish there.

The shad found in waters along the Pacific Coast — from San Diego to Alaska — is the same species as the shad on the Atlantic Coast. That's no accident. Seth Green, a fishery biologist, transplanted fry in 1871 from the Hudson River in New York to the Sacramento River in California. The shad took hold and their range expanded. As a result, today many West Coast shad fishermen think the third-generation fish in their local waters are a native species. For all the fun these anglers have with them, they might as well be. The largest shad spawning runs on the West Coast are near San Francisco and in the drainages of the Sacramento and San Joaquin river drainages. Shad are also popular (and accessible) in the American, Russian, and Feather rivers of California.

Interestingly, many shad don't share salmon's and steelhead's "one stream or nothing" attitude about spawning, for tagged fish have been found in different rivers in consecutive years. They're apparently opportunists as far as spawning goes, moving from where they are in the ocean into streams as the mood hits them. Biologists claim that the dominant motivating factor in spawning direction is water temperature. If shad are at the mouth of a river when the temperature is "right," they move inland. An awful lot of spring fly fishermen are very glad they do.

Once shad eggs hatch, the fry stay in their native streams through the summer, then drift down to the ocean for two to five years. Next they go back to the streams to spawn again. Although a variety of shad species live in most of the world's oceans, their life there remains pretty much a mystery.

For now, all fly fishermen need to know is the time the shad leave the ocean to enter the mouths of their local coastal rivers. It's a once-a-year free-for-all, where the fishermen might sometimes appear to outnumber the fish. But all that "togetherness" provides some pretty special memories, too. Thank you, Mr. Shad. (*See p. 93 for color illustration.*)

Lefty's Fly Pattern Recommendations

A tiny mouth means smaller flies — #10 to #6 are ideal for the shad. The best flies have a bit of flash or fluorescent color to them. A typical shad fly has little or no tail, a body of the smallest chenille or of thin fluorescent yarn, and a wing of calf's tail. The following combinations have been good producers over the years: chartreuse body and yellow calf's tail wing; chartreuse body and dark green calf's tail wing; fluorescent salmon-pink body and white wing; and silver Mylar body with a red or fluorescent salmon-pink wing. Recently, the tiny Clouser Minnow has been very effective on #8 or #6 long-shank hooks tied in these color combinations.

ATLANTIC PERMIT
Trachinotus falcatus

Of all the saltwater species to be taken with an artificial fly pattern, the Atlantic permit (commonly referred to simply as "permit") is probably the one that is most read about. It's a case of the impossible dream: Someone once told a fly fisherman going after permit that it couldn't be done, and the fisherman got mad, then stubborn, and hours and days and weeks of trying ultimately brought about success.

And when that first fly fisherman started taking permit . . . he found it was fun! It is a superb fly-fishing challenge, requiring study, poise, stamina, patience, and skill.

For many years, the capture of a permit on a fly was a rarity. Now it is somewhat more common, thanks primarily to the development of fly patterns that accurately mimic the shape and underwater swimming action of the crab, the permit's favorite meal. Fishing lodge operators claim their guests regularly catch permit with a fly — a bit of marketing hype that should be taken with a grain of salt — but it is fair to say that more is known today about the permit and its fly-taking habits, and more are being caught.

If you've read about permit and daydreamed about fishing for them, be assured that you can do it. There are several lodges around the world that offer reasonable rates, and even folks with limited incomes can save up for a once-in-a-lifetime trip, if that's where their daydreams lead them. Permit live in warm saltwaters, concentrating in greatest numbers, some claim, around the Florida Keys. True or not, that area provides the easiest access to the fish for most residents of the U.S.

With all the articles that have been written about the permit, it's hard to believe that every serious fly fisherman in the world doesn't know what it looks like, but for the record, here's a brief description: A permit is silver just about everywhere except for the fins, which vary from dark gray to black to dark blue, depending on the fish's age, its feeding grounds, and the time of year. Just in front of the anal fin there's a patch of yellow on the belly. The back often has a dark gray or dark blue-green shade to it, but when the fish swims over sandy bottoms grabbing small crabs, fishermen swear it's all silver, gliding in like a ghost, almost impossible to see.

The shape of a permit is unique. "Oblong with compressed sides," say biologists. "A big discus used in track meets," say the irreverent. And the fish has a blunt head, a high sloping forehead, and well-forward eyes and mouth. The dorsal and anal fins are relatively long and thin, trailing back over the body, paralleling the sharply pointed, "V"-shaped tail. As for spines, there are six of them on the first dorsal fin, and one plus around 20 soft rays on the second. There are also three spines in front of the anal fin, so be careful.

The Pacific permit (*Trachinotus kennedyi*) is found from South America's northwestern shore to California but is not as popular as its Atlantic cousin. To date, IGFA lists only Atlantic permit in its record book. All these Atlantic permit, weighing up to 40 pounds, were caught in Florida waters.

There are those who refer to some pompano as "permit" and vice versa, but that's tradition, semantics, and ignorance. Only in very small fish can identification be a problem. Remember, a permit is bigger than a pompano of the same age.

Identifying the permit is not part of the challenge — some call it obsession — that many saltwater fly fishermen have with this fish. The challenge comes, rather, from the legendary stature the permit has acquired in modern American fly fishing. More magazine articles have been written about this fish in the last 10 years than in the previous 50.

It comes, also, from the fishing experiences of our top professionals: the permit drove Joe Brooks to distraction, and it still gives Lefty Kreh apoplexy.

Of the trio of species comprising the saltwater fly-fishing grand slam, the permit is far more difficult to catch — far more — than the tarpon or bonefish.

And, for most fly fishermen, just getting the chance to make the necessary repeated casts to feeding permit is the challenge. And the daydream. *(See p. 145 for color illustration.)*

Lefty's Fly Pattern Recommendations

Only one type of fly dominates in permit fishing today, a crab pattern. Crabs are the permit's favorite food. Many crab patterns have been developed, but the two most frequently used are Del Brown's Crab Fly, often called a Merkin, and Jan Isley's Yarn Crab. Both of these flies look like crabs and sink quickly, although they are constructed of soft materials and hit the water softly. Many epoxied and heavy plastic crabs will spook the fish when they smack the surface. They can also be hard to cast.

The only other pattern that has done well on permit is the Clouser Minnow with a white underwing, chartreuse top wing, and 1/24-ounce lead eyes. For best results, this fly is thrown to the permit and manipulated constantly. The crab patterns, however, should be thrown within three feet of the fish and then allowed to sink freely.

BILLFISH

The blue, black, striped, and white marlin, plus the sailfish, spearfish, and swordfish, are commonly lumped together by most anglers under the decidedly unscientific (but nevertheless useful) term "billfish." We have elected to describe four of these seven species — the black, blue, and striped marlin, plus the sailfish. These are the billfish that are popularly fished for on a fly.

BLACK MARLIN (82)

BLUE MARLIN (86)

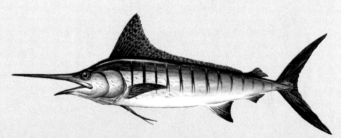

STRIPED MARLIN (87)

SAILFISH (89)

That's not to say that you couldn't catch a white marlin, a spearfish, or a swordfish on a fly, but it would be a rare event. Compared to the black, blue, and striped marlin and sailfish, the white marlin is a relatively uncommon species; and the spearfish is extremely rare. The giant swordfish is a tough brute even for hardware anglers using heavy wire leaders and electric reels. Nobody I have spoken to has ever even heard of a swordfish being hooked up, much less landed, on a fly rod. A look at the fly-rod division of the IGFA world-records reveals only one spearfish fly-rod record, and no records whatsoever for swordfish.

But if you are ambitious enough, or crazy enough, or lucky enough to encounter one of these rarely captured billfish, you should be able to distinguish and identify them quite easily. The pectoral fins of the **white marlin** are rounded, rather than pointed; the fish is generally lighter in color; and it is considerably smaller than the other marlin. The **spearfish** has a very short upper jaw or spear, and a smaller "sail" than the sailfish. And if you can't identify the extremely broad and unusual bill of the **swordfish**, you need to see your eye doctor.

BLACK MARLIN
Makaira indicus

Black marlin are generally found in tropical waters of the Pacific, from Mexico to Peru, and all the way from Japan to New Zealand. They're most numerous around islands and coastal areas.

The most distinguishing features of a black marlin are its pectoral fins, dorsal fin, and coloration. Of all the various members of the Istiophoridae family, only the black marlin has inflexible pectoral fins. These fins extend perpendicularly from the sides and cannot be bent back.

The big dorsal fin of a black marlin (technically its first dorsal fin) is shorter vertically (in proportion to the rest of the body) than that of the rest of the marlins. And the pelvic fins are usually less than 12 inches long.

The black marlin looks larger than it actually is because its body is somewhat deeper than that of other marlins and has a slight rise at the shoulder. But the black marlin's body is not rounded, so the black marlin only *seems* to be larger than a blue or striped marlin.

The back of this marlin is black or else dark slate blue (as are the fins) and it is usually devoid of stripes. The sides are pale. Light blue stripes often appear on a black marlin, and the lateral line is practically invisible, with the exception of the line on tiny fish.

A light-colored version of the black marlin which appears in the waters around Hawaii has for years been referred to as a white marlin by the locals, but the true white marlin (*Tetrapturus albidus*) is found in the Atlantic, Caribbean, and Mediterranean. Hawaii's "white marlin" is a black marlin — check the pectoral fins.

The black marlin is an important commercial fish; marlin steaks are big moneymakers. In fact, all species of marlin feed the world's human population in some significant way. The literal translation of black marlin in Japanese is "white marlin," but some suggest that refers to the color of the meat, not the flanks of the live fish.

Like all marlin, black marlin get big. The IGFA lists a fish weighing more than 1,500 pounds that was taken in 1954 off Cabo Blanco in Peru. Female marlins are larger than males; in fact, all marlin weighing over 300 pounds are females. Virtually all IGFA listings for record black marlin taken on a fly rod come from Australian waters. The largest fish weighed 94 pounds, taken on a 16-pound-test tippet, and the 8-pound-tippet fish weighed 46 pounds. That's a small fish, but it's a small tippet class, too. The 2 and 4-pound-test categories have not been filled yet (surprise, surprise). Looks like there's room for new records.

Lastly, here's a bit of trivia for all lovers of marlin. When his book *The Old Man and the Sea* was being made into a movie, Ernest Hemingway (a big blue marlin fan) served as a technical consultant and tried to arrange for the fishing shots to take place in his favorite Cuban waters. When that didn't work out because of the fish's seasonal migration, the entire film crew went to Peru. So what you see in the movie are *black* marlin off Peru, not Hemingway's *blue* marlin off Cuba. If your daydreams of marlin fishing are built on scenes in that movie, you're thinking about black marlin.

On the other hand, if your daydreams come from pleasant memories of black marlin you've already caught . . . you're lucky. *(See p. 81 for color illustration.)*

Lefty's Fly Pattern Recommendations
Some fly fishermen feel that the most exciting species you can catch are billfish — marlin and sailfish. It's thrilling to see a six-foot-long fish within 20 feet of the transom and know it may take your fly.

Much has been written about the best billfish flies. However, those anglers who have had the good fortune to catch a number of billfish feel that once a marlin or sailfish has been excited and drawn to the boat, it will eat virtually any fly that comes in its direction. I agree. But there are a few things to consider when selecting a billfish fly.

Australian fly fishermen — who have had more experience than anyone trying to catch very large billfish on flies — feel that a fly needs to be no longer than eight inches, provided the fish has been properly teased to the boat. Anglers who throw 12 to 15-inch flies at larger billfish may be wasting their energy. Most billfish flies are either a form of a large Lefty's

Deceiver (six to nine inches long), or a streamer fly of the same length. Some anglers believe that the color of the fly is important, but my experience and the experience of others indicate that this is not the case.

What is important is that your fly carry two hooks in tandem — the principal hook in front, usually a #3/0 to #5/0, and a smaller stringer hook in back, usually a #3/0. Most fly tyers place the principal hook in front in the normal attitude (with the bend of the hook below the shank), and the back stringer hook in the opposite orientation (with the bend of the hook above the shank), so that the two hooks, while facing in the same direction, are on two parallel planes, 180 degrees from each other. However, the Australians have discovered that the orientation of the stringer hook to the principal hook should not be 180 but about 90 degrees, or, in other words, offset to the side. This is because when the fish grabs a tandem fly with both hooks oriented on parallel planes, the two hooks can slither through its closed jaw. To test this, tie a tandem fly with one hook above its shank and the other below its shank. Place it inside the pages of a book and close the book. You'll find this tandem fly can be pulled from the pages. But if the stringer hook is offset from the principal hook at an angle of about 90 degrees, this offset hook will dig into the pages.

Most experienced billfish anglers recommend a slide-on popping head. Before the streamer fly has been tied on the bite leader, a one-inch-long, soft, flexible, round rod of plastic foam (many fishermen prefer Ethafoam) is shoved over the hook eye. When retrieved, this foam rod will pop and gurgle, attracting the fish's attention to the fly. It is advisable to secure the plastic rod to the head, since this rod can slip up on the tippet during a fight. On two occasions, I have had smaller fish with sharp teeth attack the plastic rod and bite the leader in half.

BLUE MARLIN
Makaira nigricans

This is it, folks! They just don't get any bigger and better than the blue marlin. Top floor. Watch your step getting off.

Zane Grey and Ernest Hemingway went gaga over these critters, and so have a lot of men and women who apparently have more money than demands on their time. For well over 50 years, stories have circulated about people being bitten by the blue marlin bug and never returning to the office.

Record books list fish weighing in excess of 1,500 pounds being taken on rod and reel. To date, it hasn't happened with a fly rod, but the puny existing records of 150 to 200 pounds can inspire fishermen bitten by the bug. The *potential* is there to catch a 300 or 400-pound blue marlin on a fly rod. Somebody's gotta be the first, they say. Why not *me?!?!*

Blue marlin are in the Atlantic and Pacific oceans and move around seasonally, looking for cooler water in the summer and warmer water in the winter. Remember that there are two sides to the equator. Marlin can go north or south for their summer vacations, so there are good populations of blue marlin somewhere in the world every month of the year. Mind-boggling, isn't it?

Check your favorite warm-water seaside hideaway; chances are, blue marlin are nearby at least 60 days of the year. They're found from Cape Cod to Florida and down the South American coast to Uruguay, also from northern Mexico (sometimes even Southern California) to Peru. They live in the eastern Atlantic from France to South Africa, in the Indian Ocean, and around Hawaii, Japan, and New Zealand. This big daydream is *accessible*. (I didn't say the access was cheap.)

A blue marlin is cobalt or steely blue on its back, white on its belly, and silvery white with light blue or lavender stripes on its sides. The body is quite tubular and doesn't taper down in the back as noticeably as the body of a black or striped marlin. Unlike those of the black marlin, the blue's pectoral fins can be bent back along its body, even after the fish is dead. The dorsal fin is relatively large, not huge, as is the pointed anal fin. Both are usually dark blue.

The bill of the upper jaw is not as flat as the bill on other marlins; instead, it is almost oval. The lower jaw stops growing once the blue marlin reaches maturity, but the upper jaw keeps getting longer. A 300 to 800-pound blue marlin has a truly impressive bill.

The increase in popularity of blue marlin tournaments has led many tournament sponsors to develop a "tag-and-release" policy, and some government agencies are taking advantage of these tagging programs for their research projects. The IGFA, which has a tag-and-release category, is among those encouraging release of these magnificent creatures of the sea. Hopefully, stuffed billfish hanging on office and den walls are a thing of the past. They'd better be, if our grandchildren are to have the same opportunity we do for catching a 200-pound blue marlin on a fly rod.

Think about that for a while. Sort of explains what Zane and Ernest were excited about, doesn't it? (*See p. 81 for color illustration.*)

Lefty's Fly Pattern Recommendations
See Black Marlin.

STRIPED MARLIN
Tetrapturus audax

Striped marlin are smaller than blacks or blues, but they make up for it with their fighting characteristics. People who have caught them say they seemingly spend more time in the air than the water once hooked. They run, tail-walk, skitter across the surface, and have been known to make as many as a dozen graceful leaps in a row, all of them powering away from the angler and his boat.

Two fly-rod world records for striped marlin were made off the coast of Ecuador. One fish was caught in 1967, the other in 1970, and each weighed just under 150 pounds. Several 200 to 400-pound fish have been caught on conventional gear, so catching a 50 to 200-pound striped marlin on a fly rod is a realistic possibility.

If you go after this striped marlin, you'll likely spend most of your time in either the Pacific or Indian oceans — the striped marlin is caught off the coasts of California, Chile, Peru, Ecuador, Japan, Australia, and New Zealand, and in all the warm to temperate waters in between.

Gratefully for anglers, the striped marlin tends to do most of its feeding, fighting, and sunbathing on the surface and close to shore. It is the one species of marlin that is probably more accessible to the angler in a sportfishing boat than to the deep-water commercial fisherman. Add this accessibility to the way it fights on the hook, and you will understand why this fish is so popular worldwide.

The striped marlin's dorsal fin is usually as long as its body is high, and the front tip is tapered, as are the tips of the pectoral and anal fins. The pectoral fins are flat, curved, and proportionally large, and can be bent back against the fish's body, like those of the blue marlin. The bill is relatively long compared to the length of the fish's body. You can see the lateral line on some striped marlin, a nearly straight, single line of dots running from just behind the gill plate to the tail. The fish has slab (flat) sides like the black marlin that narrow towards the back.

The fish was undoubtedly named for the stripes on its sides, for it has more visible vertical stripes than a blue or black marlin. These markings are generally pale blue, pale purple, or white, and their visibility varies among individual fish. Identification tip: If you think you have a striped marlin but the stripes are very pale or obscured, look for large dorsal and pectoral fins and a large bill.

Overall, the striped marlin is dark blue on the back, paling to near white on the belly. The dorsal and anal fins are often bright blue and the rest of the fins are dark blue or black. On some fish there are spots on the lower part of the body and on the larger fins. Biologists say a striped marlin's coloration will vary a great deal depending upon where the fish is living and what feed is available. In fact, some people who have studied or fished for striped marlin in the same waters over long periods of time claim they can determine when migrating fish are moving in just by their coloration.

How would it be to fish one piece of warm saltwater for so many years that you could be able to tell when migrating marlin were coming through? Oh, sweet daydreams. *(See p. 81 for color illustration.)*

Lefty's Fly Pattern Recommendations
See Black Marlin.

SAILFISH
Istiophorus platyperus

Sailfish are probably one of the more dramatic gamefish that can be taken with a fly and fly rod. Their huge, cobalt-blue dorsal fin and long, pointed bill make them easily identifiable, but it's their fighting characteristics that make sailfish memorable. Experienced billfish fishermen like fighting sailfish because these fish are so acrobatic and active . . . for a reasonably short period of time. Anglers won't die of a heart attack fighting a sailfish. (They might die of giddiness, but not cardiac arrest.)

A sailfish is long and thin with flat sides; a 40-pound fish may be six feet long. The back is usually dark blue, the belly white or silver, and the sides are often bronze. Spaced quite evenly down the sides is a series of light blue lines, each line consisting of thin vertical ovals nearly touching each other. The visible lateral line runs straight down the side on a mature sailfish.

The pelvic fins, up front on the lower side of the fish, are very unique to the sailfish. They're thin and long approaching the anal fin, and they are connected by a membrane that is very conspicuous on a live fish. The pectoral fins are also quite elongated and can be bent back against the body like those of some marlin species.

The "sail" of the sailfish is the first dorsal fin, which is always 1 1/2 to two times as deep as the body and runs most of the fish's length. This fin is ragged on top, dipping and rising erratically from front to back, peaking in the last third of its length, and terminating above the anal fin. The second dorsal and anal fins are cobalt blue like the sail, but lack its black dots. The fish's second dorsal is very short, beginning well back of the sail.

The sailfish is found in tropical waters of the Atlantic, Pacific, and Indo-Pacific oceans. There are quite a few fish off the Florida coast in December and January, and some sailfish are found from Baja California to Ecuador in the Pacific all year long. Reports of sailfish being caught around Korea, New Zealand, Australia, and Hawaii have been confirmed. Of the 10 current fly-rod records listed with IGFA, nine fish were caught in the 1980s and 1990s in Cozumel and Cancún, Mexico, in Senegal, and in Costa Rica. The tenth, a 136-pounder caught off Panama in 1965, was taken by one of Lefty Kreh's close friends, Stu Apte.

For all the scientific studies this fish has generated, biologists are quick to point out there's a lot they don't know. Some of them expect further research will show that the Atlantic sailfish, having the same species name as the larger Pacific sailfish, is capable of growing as large as its Pacific counterpart. Other scientists disagree, and look forward to the day when at least three separate species or subspecies of sailfish will be recognized in all scientific and sporting publications. Despite all the fishing, chasing, and catching going on, experienced saltwater fly fishermen say there's a lot they don't know about the sailfish, either.

One thing is certain, however. Watching a seven-foot fish with a four-foot sail over its back rise to your fly is *definitely* sport — and fun! *(See p. 81 for color illustration.)*

Lefty's Fly Pattern Recommendations
See Black Marlin.

BLUEFISH
Pomatomus saltatrix

Many consider the bluefish the toughest, meanest, and therefore best gamefish there is in either salt or freshwater. That's quite a statement, but it's heard from so many anglers of sound reputation that it has to be taken seriously. John Hersey wrote an entire book about the fish (and a whole lot more) in *Blues,* a work every bluefish angler should read. It captures the essence of fishing for bluefish, including what most fishermen don't think about very often — namely, why *they* are out there after the blues.

A bluefish *is* indeed sort of blue — blue green on the back and sides, gradually fading to white, the fins pretty much matching the body. At the start of each pectoral fin is a patch of black. The first dorsal fin is low and short with six to eight spines; this fin is less than half the length of the second. On some fish, the second dorsal fin has one spine and 25 to 27 soft rays; others have no spines and fewer than 25 soft rays.

The fish is a little chunky with a somewhat tapered snout and a protruding bottom jaw. Its large mouth is full of tremendously sharp canine teeth which, thanks to the fish's being able to focus while out of water, have cost a few fishermen their fingers. The bluefish snaps so constantly that it's called a snapper when small, and sometimes a chopper or marine piranha later in its life. If you know nothing about the bluefish, it's easy to figure out what this fish is known for from those nicknames.

The bluefish is not big; record-book fish weigh less than 20 pounds. Many fishermen catch five-pound fish and are happy (but most are a lot happier with 10 or 15-pounders, however). This is powerful testimony to the fish's fighting capabilities.

Bluefish live in temperate or tropically warm waters throughout the world, with (fortunately for fishermen) a sizable population off the Eastern Seaboard of the U.S., where huge schools of blues migrate up and down the coast during the year. For a long time, bluefish were believed to reach Florida shores in the winter and then move up the coast to Maine as the water warmed during the summer. Now some scientists say they come in directly from clear water, traveling until they reach the shorelines where baitfish are prevalent. But whether they head south to north or east to west makes little difference to the angler, who knows that the blues come in cycles and the best time to fish for them is whenever they're feeding just offshore.

Fishermen have long claimed that certain oil slicks on the surface of the water were signs of bluefish on the feed. Not only that, they also noticed a cucumber or melon smell in the

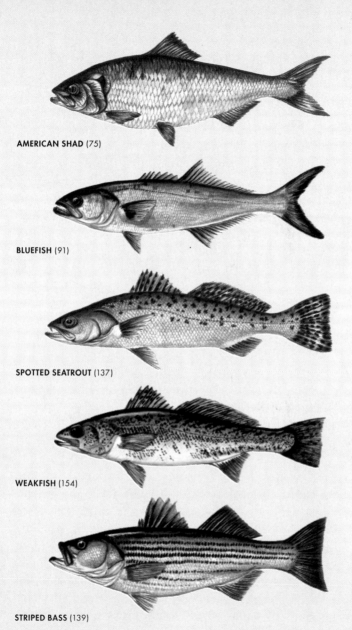

AMERICAN SHAD (75)

BLUEFISH (91)

SPOTTED SEATROUT (137)

WEAKFISH (154)

STRIPED BASS (139)

area. Researchers now tell us it's the smell of plankton in the air, released from the thousands of baitfish being devoured or injured by bluefish. Scientific and accurate perhaps, but it sure takes some of the mystique away from fishing for blues.

There's no mistaking feeding bluefish; their ferocity and aggressive runs are legendary. Fishermen from Massachusetts to South Carolina tell stories of frenzied blues chasing baitfish right up to the beach and then beaching themselves in one last frantic lunge.

In the last decade, fly rods have begun showing up on the Atlantic Coast beside the surf-casting rods. Obviously, some-one must be having success with the "long rod." Fly fisher-men have gone to city parks and reservoirs to practice casting greater distances . . . just so they can reach a bluefish while they're wading in the surf.

Friends from cities all up and down the East Coast form "bluefish networks." The lucky person living next to the ocean calls five or six designated fishermen when the bluefish are just offshore and feeding, these people in turn call others, and cars and trucks, with tackle already packed, are soon filled like fire engines. The "run" from the cities to the shoreline rivals the run offshore.

Bluefish bring out the best in people. *(See p. 93 for color illustration.)*

Lefty's Fly Pattern Recommendations

I've heard it said that the bluefish is always hungry, but there are times when it can be very reluctant to strike. The surest way to catch a bluefish on a fly is in a chum line, and if ground chum is used, the Chum Fly Bloody is terrific. This is a simple fly to tie: Just wrap the hook shank with a few turns of lead wire, and then surround the hook with a skirt no longer than 1 1/2 inches made of dark brown marabou. That's it! Fish it in the chum line without manipulating it — you want the fly to drift just as the ground pieces of chum are drifting. It's a little like fishing nymphs for trout.

Popping bugs work well on a bluefish, although the life of the bugs is short under the fish's teeth. If the bluefish is breaking on the surface, almost any fly you get to it will be taken. When it's basking on the surface, it can be very spooky, and on those occasions a good baitfish imitation is suggested, with a long leader and no more than four inches of wire bite tippet. Hook sizes for the bluefish range from #1 to #3/0.

BONEFISH
Albula vulpes

The bonefish is probably fly fishing's ultimate gamefish on the saltwater flats. It is an aquatic chameleon — white over sand, green over turtle grass, pale blue or polished silver in the light — identified only by its black eyes, the pattern of dark spots and stripes on its upper body, and the motion of the water above, called "nervous water."

The bonefish is the sole survivor of its genus and family, and an ancient and primitive family it is. The Albulidae were among the first bony fishes that lived during the Cretaceous geological period.

The fish is sleek and slim with a pointed head and a definite snout, its mouth tucked slightly back and under. Like most saltwater fish, the bonefish is amazingly compact; it's a rare fish that's over two feet long. As far as fly-fishing records are concerned, no bonefish has ever been taken weighing more than 15 pounds, and that's with six leader categories ranging from two to 20-pound-test. It's a very solid fish. Most fishermen catching the usual 10-pound bonefish will be surprised that something that "small" can run off so much line and backing in such a short time.

The Atlantic bonefish's home range is the coastal waters south of the Carolinas clear to Brazil. Pacific bonefish range off Northern California to Peru. But most bonefish are found in warm, tropical seas: those around Florida, Mexico, Central and South America, the Bahamas, West Africa, and the coral atolls of the South Pacific.

The adult spends its life drifting in and out with the tides. It follows rising tides onto the flats for the shrimp, mollusks, crabs, squid, sea worms, and smaller fish it finds there. Once on the flats, it usually feeds snout-down. The wary nature of this fish, always on the lookout for danger, is what attracts sport fishermen. To catch a bonefish in shallow water on foot (sometimes on knees) or in a small skiff is a definite challenge. Sure, a little human ego comes into play here, but that's another issue.

I'd like to finish with a few words by the late Harry Middleton, noted author, passionate fisherman, and friend to many, Lefty Kreh and myself included. Here's a little of what Harry said about bonefish in a companion volume in the Library, *Fly Fishing for Bonefish, Permit & Tarpon:*

"From an angling standpoint, there are no fish on the flats that are easy. There are only challenges of differing degrees of difficulty, bonefish being among the most difficult species to stalk and capture. Bonefish are wary and suspicious, shy, and yet, once hooked, they are among the most tenacious fish in the sea, creatures of deep and uncorrupted spirit, the essence of wildness. . . .

"Capturing a bonefish on a fly then becomes a matter first of avoiding its close attention, and then of tempting its rapacious hunger.

"Bonefish can be stalked only if they can be found. In the extremes of most saltwater flats, with their harsh sunlight and wind, concentration becomes all important. An angler must learn to look not at the water, but through it, learning the bottom, the shape and movements of squid and rays, sharks and boxfish, crabs and shrimp, turtle grass and shifting sand. Knowing what is natural to the flat makes it a little easier to pick up a milling bonefish or the sudden appearance of something that is an anomaly, like the thin sickle silhouette of the back, tail, or fin of a tailing fish. The experienced bonefisher suspects every wrinkle of nervous water, every disturbance of mud, silt, sand. It could be a bonefish. And if the fates are kind, it could be the presence of not one bonefish but a small school, all of them preoccupied, momentarily unaware." (*See p. 145 for color illustration.*)

Lefty's Fly Pattern Recommendations

Studies have shown that the bonefish will eat anything it can get into its mouth and swallow. Since the mouth of even a large, 10-pound bonefish is rather small, flies need to be small, too. I have noticed in my nearly 30 years of fishing for bonefish that as soon as someone makes several bonefish trips, he often develops a deadly bonefish lure, touting it as the fly to end all flies. Since fly fishing is supposed to be fun, I never burst his balloon. But the truth is, if flies are presented properly, a bonefish will strike just about any reasonable pattern. *Most of the time, flies that match the bottom color are best. On white, sandy flats, light-colored flies will generally do well, and on darker flats, flies a bit darker are usually recommended.* Common sense should tell you that any bonefish prey whose color contrasts markedly with the ocean bottom would have been gobbled up long ago.

After trying literally hundreds of fly patterns, I have reduced my choice of flies to just a few. For flies with lead eyes, I simply tie on the lead eyes and a wing, leaving the hook shank free of any sort of body dressing. These flies strike the water more softly, and the fish accepts them just as well as any more fully dressed patterns made today.

I would be content to fish with about a half-dozen patterns the rest of my life, for I've learned through experience that if I present these flies properly, the fish generally will be hooked. Three flies I would never go after bonefish without are two color combinations of the Clouser Minnow and the Gotcha. Both of the Clousers have a white underwing, and either a chartreuse or very light tan upper wing. The Gotcha is nothing more than a white Crazy Charlie with an extra-long, pink nose. It seems to outfish all other Crazy Charlie patterns for me. I would add two more patterns: the Mini-Puff in light and dark colors, and the brown Snapping Shrimp.

For bonefish under four pounds, I like to use #6 or #4 hooks. For larger bonefish, a #4 or #2 hook is preferred. When you bring along the flies that I've listed above, you can fish confidently, knowing you have at least one of the right patterns for bonefish in your box.

BONITO
Sarda sarda, Sarda chiliensis, Sarda orientalis

The words "bonito" and "bonita" mean "pretty" or "beautiful" in Spanish. This may not seem to have much to do with *Sarda sarda*, the Atlantic bonito, *Sarda chiliensis*, the Pacific or California bonito, or *Sarda orientalis*, the striped bonito, also a Pacific fish — except that a whole lot of people pronounce the name of this magnificent fish as if it ended in "a" instead of "o," driving writers and editors crazy. It's *bonito*, folks, not bonita! But pretty is pretty in any language, and whoever has the opportunity to fly fish for this beautiful creature is fortunate.

Those who know bonito know that they're ocean-dwelling, roaming members of the mackerel family (Scombridae), a family which includes wahoo, various tunas and mackerels,

ATLANTIC BONITO (98)

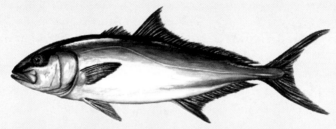

GREATER AMBERJACK (109)

ATLANTIC SPANISH MACKEREL (119)

NASSAU GROUPER (112)

albacore, and one species of mackerel called cero, which, phonetically, is Spanish for "zero." Which sort of gets us back to where we started.

The bonito is not a large fish; an eight to 10-pounder is considered big, and most are two to three feet long. The IGFA fly-fishing record book lists just four Atlantic bonito, leaving two categories still vacant; and five Pacific bonito, with just the 20-pound-test category still vacant. The largest of the two species recorded are a 10-pounder from the Atlantic and a 15-pounder from the Pacific.

So if it's not size that makes the bonito irresistible, what is it? Let's go back to the name, "pretty." The back is steel blue or blue green and the lower sides and flanks are silvery. Above the lateral line, dark stripes angle up the sides until they meet the dark coloration of the back. On most species, the stripes are a little wavy, sometimes irregular, and on others, they are relatively straight and solid. All in all, the coloration and pattern are simply . . . beautiful.

No bonito in American waters has stripes covering the lower half of its body, but there is an Australian bonito that does. To really confuse the issue, there's a third American-waters bonito, the striped bonito, *Sarda orientalis*, that shares parts of the Pacific coastline with the Pacific bonito. Its stripes are just on the upper portion of its sides and back. A series of longitudinal, oblique lines on the upper side of the bonito distinguish it from close relatives like the skipjack tuna, which has stripes only on the bottom half of its body and is, incidentally, a considerably larger fish. Three species of little tunny also look like the bonito, except that tunny are usually somewhat smaller and have a tall first dorsal fin.

A bonito's first dorsal fin is triangular but not tall. There are between 20 and 23 spines in this fin on the Atlantic bonito, and only 17 to 22 on the Pacific and striped bonito. The second dorsal fin on a bonito has just 13 to 18 rays, followed by six to eight finlets. This should be enough identification help for record seekers.

Experienced saltwater fly fishermen know they may sometimes have to go 15 or 20 miles offshore for them, but if bonito are up on the surface slashing on baitfish, there's a good chance of hooking up using a minnow imitation. Bonito leap and skip across the water when they're feeding — and they leap and skip even more once they feel steel. They're some of the most exciting of our saltwater gamefish.

The Atlantic bonito is found throughout the Atlantic Ocean and the Mediterranean and Black Seas. There's a definite gap in its territory — namely, the Gulf of Mexico and the Caribbean — and no one knows why. The Pacific bonito divides its territory into a northern beat, from British Columbia to southern Baja California; and a South American one, along Peru and Chile. This leaves another mysterious gap, to be filled in by the striped bonito which inhabits waters from Baja California to Peru. These strange, disconnected territories mean a large area for any fisherman to go after these beautiful fish. *(See p. 99 for color illustration.)*

Lefty's Fly Pattern Recommendations

Rarely does a bonito feed on baitfish that are longer than 3 1/2 inches, so the streamer flies used for this fish are generally from 1 1/2 to 2 1/2 inches long. Sparsely tied patterns usually produce better than more fully dressed flies. Just a little bit of flash is added — too much Flashabou or Crystal Flash can often spoil the presentation.

Good patterns are small Clouser Minnows, usually dressed with Ultra Hair because that material is translucent, with just a few strands of Crystal Flash added. The lower portion of the wing is generally pale white or smoke, and the upper wing is usually smoke, gray, pale blue, or pale green. The smaller version of the Surf Candy pattern is also effective.

COBIA
Rachycentron canadum

The cobia is a saltwater gamefish found in tropical and warm waters all over the world. It is an interesting species in several ways. For one thing, the cobia gets *big!* The record books list cobia weighing more than 100 pounds, and even on fly rods, two over 60 pounds and another over 80 pounds have been caught and registered. A 100-pound cobia is more than five feet long. That's something to dream about.

Because of its size, among other things, the cobia can be seen quite easily when it's surface-feeding close to shore. Casters have been known to race up and down the edge on dune buggies in order to get close to feeding cobia. Sounds a bit like "chasing blues," doesn't it?

Another interesting aspect of the cobia is its appearance and the comments it generates from anglers. Although they are the only members of the family Rachycentridae, with a distinctive shape (tapered at both ends with a protruding lower jaw), cobia remind fishermen of other species. Some say the cobia looks like a shark, or a remora, or a whiskerless catfish! This latter reference is undoubtedly due to the cobia's coloration — a dark chocolate brown on the top of its body which gradually fades to lighter shades of brown on the sides and near white on the bottom or belly. Also, the cobia has tiny scales — giving it the "feel" of a catfish.

Why the cobia is also frequently mistaken for a shark and the shark's companion fish, the remora, is probably because the cobia occupies, more often than not, the same area of the ocean as these two species, following along behind these fish to pick up leftovers from the shark's predation.

There are ways to distinguish the cobia from other species, however. The lateral line is black, continuous and wavy, and the pectoral fins are relatively large, usually dark brown or black. The front dorsal fin is made up of eight to 10 unconnected spines (and therefore not considered a fin by most fishermen). The more significant dorsal fin is quite large and long, the front extending high enough to break water like a shark's fin, another cause for confusion. This fin and the anal fin are sort of mirror images, the top fin darker and farther to the front. The head is elongated, depressed, and broad, somewhat like that of a catfish.

Cobia can be found in U.S. waters from Massachusetts to Florida and over to Bermuda, also in the Gulf of Mexico, off Argentina's northern shores, and around Australia. Another species has apparently now taken over the waters off California and Mexico's western shore, for cobia were formerly not found in this part of the Pacific.

Off the coasts of the United States, cobia seem to prefer the continental shelf, gathering around anything that floats or sticks out of the water — buoys, channel markers, wrecks, pilings, oil rigs, or anchored ships. However, when the fish are hooked around such structures, line cutoffs are common.

Since they like warm water, cobia only live in the northern parts of their range during the summer months; all of the U.S. records for cobia caught on a fly rod were achieved in Florida waters. Still, if you hear of cobia off the coastline you know best, give them a try. The cobia is a fighter, making powerful runs and occasionally leaping clear of the water. And a big fish on a fly rod is always a good combination anywhere. When's the last time you cast your fly to a 60-pound fish?

Think cobia. *(See p. 149 for color illustration.)*

Lefty's Fly Pattern Recommendations

Few fish fight harder than the cobia. A small cobia, less than 25 pounds, is an avid eater and will take almost any streamer fly or popping bug. But a larger cobia wants a big meal, and small flies and poppers hold little interest. For a cobia of this size, you need to fish very large streamers, such as the 10 or 12-inch style that I describe in the striped bass section. However, I have had more success in attracting cobia larger than 40 pounds with a big popping bug. A bug with a face the size of a quarter is ideal, producing such a disturbance that a large cobia thinks it's come upon a very good meal.

DOLPHIN
Coryphaena hippurus

The dolphin (*the fish — not the mammal which bears the same name*) is probably the most brightly colored fish discussed in this book. Dolphin live well offshore in warm-water seas throughout the world.

Identification of a mature dolphin is simple. It's shaped like a torpedo, and has flat sides, a big head, markedly tapered body, and a mid-sized, extremely forked tail. The dorsal fin runs almost the entire length of the back, from above the eye to just short of the tail. The front of the head of a mature male (bull) dolphin extends almost vertically up from its mouth.

The back of a live dolphin in the water is a beautiful iridescent blue or blue green. Its sides are silvery gold, bluish gold, or all gold, and its belly silvery white or yellow. There's a mix of dark and light colored spots scattered down the flanks, some black, some blue, others golden. The dorsal fin is rich blue, the anal fin is golden or silvery, and the rest of the fins are often golden, edged in blue.

When a dolphin is hooked, all these colors seem to become fluorescent, flashing on and off and changing hues, like those of billfish. When fighting a hook and line, a dolphin often shows dark vertical bands on its sides.

Dolphin are caught off southern U.S. shores on the Atlantic and Pacific Coasts but are more common off Baja California, Mexico, and Central America, in the Caribbean, and around Japan and Australia. Occasionally a few dolphin will swim up with the Gulf Stream as far north as Prince Edward Island. They usually go no farther north than Los Angeles. They are prevalent around Japan and Australia. In Hawaii, they're call *mahi-mahi*.

A bull dolphin is generally larger than a female, and the bull's big head helps distinguish it from the female, whose head is rounder. A smaller species called the pompano dolphin (*Coryphaena equiselis*) is sometimes mistaken for its bigger cousin, but it's easy to tell apart even the immature of both species. The pompano dolphin is more squat, especially in the midsection, and its dorsal fins start well back of the eye, almost in the middle of the back.

Record-sized dolphin on a fly rod weigh over 50 pounds. The all-time record fish weigh more than 70 pounds and measure over five feet long. Most fly fishermen catch fish in the five to 25-pound range at resorts catering to the species. Many of these resorts are now beginning to promote the catch-and-release ethic, which may be part of the reason why more 35 to 45-pound bull dolphin are being caught than ever before. Many experienced saltwater fishermen feel that, pound for pound, the dolphin strikes and fights harder than the sailfish, marlin, or tuna.

The dolphin feeds on flying fish and other species that hide in sargassum seaweed. Many an angler has seen terrified flying fish leap from the water, sail 50 or 75 feet — and fall into the mouth of a dolphin who's been following its favorite food for its entire flight. This is one of sportfishing's great sights.

And offshore, when you're casting into the middle of a feeding frenzy, there's no mistaking the rod-wrenching strike of a dolphin. A high-leaping fish ripping line off your reel burns images in your mind. It's a fly-fishing moment that all should experience. (*See p. 149 for color illustration.*)

Few fish take flies better than a dolphin, which hits both streamers and poppers. Most of the time, a streamer fly that is weighted reaches a school faster. The best color combination for me by far has been a yellow body with a red head or collar. The Lefty's Deceiver, with a yellow wing, lots of gold Flashabou on each side, and a red collar of bucktail, is dynamite. I hate to keep mentioning the Clouser Minnow, but this fly, loaded with heavy lead eyes, a long yellow wing, and a short red wing at the front, is also very effective. Streamer flies that imitate local baitfish are always a good bet, as are popping bugs, especially on a slick sea. The color of the bug appears to be unimportant.

GREAT BARRACUDA
Sphyraena barracuda

According to textbooks, the barracuda we all know and love is not just a barracuda — it's a *great* barracuda, or *Sphyraena barracuda*. What saltwater fly fishermen know about the barracuda is substantial: It's considered one of the best gamefish available, with a vicious bite, a voracious strike, and long, leaping runs that eat up backing in a moment. A closer look is definitely in order.

The barracuda is regarded, by the non-fishing public in particular, as a dangerous fish — an aggressive critter ready to take a bite out of you. Those who often fish for barracuda or swim with them say this is a bum rap, just as it is for the South American piranha. The barracuda is more curious than dangerous, but fishermen and snorkelers do admit that the bite of a barracuda is pretty mean. People who have seen the bite say a barracuda's is straight and clean, unlike the round and jagged bite of a shark.

Indeed, it's the teeth of barracuda that get all the media attention. Basically, barracuda have a mouth full of canines — the rear teeth are all quite vertical, and only the teeth toward the front of the upper and lower jaws are angled back. Or to put it another way, that's one design for slashing, another for holding. Always efficient, Mother Nature left her mark when she designed the barracuda.

The most obvious physical characteristic of a barracuda is its shape — long and lean, a little like an elongated, sea-going silver pike. The long, slim body is attached to a pointed head, the lower jaw extending slightly beyond the upper jaw. The body is dull to bright silver with a pale belly and a back of bluish gray (sometimes dark green). On the sides there are grayish black blotches here and there, also a few entirely black irregular blotches, particularly toward the tail.

Many first time " 'cuda chasers" confuse the barracuda with a bonefish, especially in shallow waters, like a mangrove shore. Experienced fishermen tell these novices to watch for movement. A bonefish is always moving, but a barracuda will often lie dead still in the water, only its shadow providing a means of identification.

Since small sharks — like the lemon, shovelnose, nurse, and blacktip — frequent the same waters as barracuda, inexperienced fishermen sometimes also mistake a small shark for a barracuda. Again, the experienced fishermen have counsel: watch the tail. A shark's tail moves back and forth quite a bit and you'll see side-to-side body movement as the tail moves. When a barracuda decides to move, all you'll see is the speed of its exit.

The great barracuda is found in Atlantic waters from northern Florida to Brazil and from the Bahamas to the Virgin Islands. Some scientists recognize as many as 20 smaller species of barracuda in Atlantic waters but only one in the Pacific. The Pacific barracuda, *Sphyraena argentea*, has a limited range from central California southward, including most of the length of the Baja Peninsula in California.

To identify a great barracuda, look for five spines in the first dorsal fin and 10 soft rays in both the second dorsal and the anal fins. And for a bit of trivia, if you take the anal fin or second dorsal fin and push the long soft ray at the leading edge of the fin back over the nine behind it so that they are flush with the body of the fish, the lead soft ray is long enough to cover the nine other soft rays. Who cares, you might ask? Folks seeking world records, that's who. If you can't identify a fish, you can't claim it.

And claiming world barracuda records has attracted a lot of attention lately. Four of the six saltwater fly-rod world records have been entered since 1990. Most of the trophy fish weighed less than 40 pounds; only one, caught off Christmas Island, was in the 60 to 80-pound range. Four of the six fish were caught in Florida waters.

While size and length are crucial to record seekers, they don't seem as important to sport fishermen, many of whom are content with three to eight-pound barracuda. And while record seekers look for 'cudas five or six feet long, most fly fishermen simply try to match their rod and line weights to the size fish they are encountering.

Fun is where you find it, they say, and if you can find barracuda with a fly rod in your hand . . . ya done good! And you are going to have fun. Enjoy yourself. That's what it's all about. *(See p. 145 for color illustration.)*

Lefty's Fly Pattern Recommendations

For many years, fly fishermen felt the best way to catch a barracuda was to present a fly resembling a needlefish and then strip it as fast as possible. This worked, but all too often the swift 'cuda would rush the fly, look at it, and turn away. I have long since stopped using needlefish imitations because, in my opinion, I don't believe they offer enough "meat" to excite a large barracuda. Besides that, the long, sleek wing of the fly is always getting tangled in flight on the cast, spoiling many presentations.

The technique I now use doesn't always work but is more effective than anything else I've tried. I drop a fly three feet in front of the barracuda and then immediately make a long, smooth back cast (or single water haul). The 'cuda either runs away or is excited by the fly that touches down, zips in front of it — and then disappears. I repeat the cast, simply drop the fly on the water, pull it slowly in front of the fish, and then lift it again for another back cast. If I can see that the 'cuda is definitely determined to hit this thing, then I'll drop the fly three feet in front of the fish and make a slow retrieve to swim the fly.

Aside from this technique, catching a barracuda all depends on the type of fly used. I prefer one particular pattern tied in two different color combinations. Put a long shank hook (#1/0 to #3/0) upside down in the vise and tie on a liberal supply of bucktail wing, the longest you can get. Turn the hook over and attach 10 to 20 strands of gold Flashabou half an inch longer than the wing. Then tie in more bucktail on top of the Flashabou so that you have a full "skirt" of bucktail surrounding the hook. For this fly, I either use all orange or white for the underwing and chartreuse for the upperwing.

GREATER AMBERJACK
Seriola dumerili

The amberjack is an ocean dweller, a member of the Carangidae family, which includes roosterfish, permit, jacks, scads, pompanos, and lookdowns. That's fast company, and a quick look at an amberjack shows it's built for speed. Add that to the fact that it'll hit a fly like a freight train and then proceed to take off like one, and you have a fish very popular with fly fishermen.

If you were to make a simple line drawing of an amberjack, you could start out with the graceful Christian fish symbol you often see on bumper stickers. The elongated oval and the distinct, "V"-shaped tail of that symbol are very similar to the shape of the amberjack.

And the amberjack is not just beautiful — it gets big. Stories of amberjack four and five feet long and weighing well over 100 pounds capture interest. IGFA saltwater fly-rod world records list just one fish over 100 pounds, one at 80, and several between 10 and 30 pounds. Most of the latter are very recent records, set in the early 1990s. That means amberjack are drawing the attention of more and more fly fishermen.

Unlike the rest of the Carangidae family, the amberjack has an elongated (and usually thicker) body and no scutes in the lateral line. The first dorsal fin has seven to eight spines, and the anal fin is considerably shorter than the dorsal.

Most scientists recognize 12 species of amberjack, four genera, in American waters. Some recognize a few more species in the Mediterranean or elsewhere. Clearly the most popular is the greater amberjack, *Seriola dumerili*, largest and most important of the seven species of amberjack that call the Atlantic Ocean home.

The greater amberjack is generally brown, olive, or deep blue on top, and silver and white along the bottom of the belly, especially toward the rear of the fish. A dark olive diagonal stripe stretches from the mouth and across the eye, stopping at about the first dorsal fin. The rest of the fish is mostly olive, except along the sides, where a band of amber (hence the name), often mixed with gold and lavender, extends from eye to tail. It's a beautiful combination of colors that makes a truly beautiful fish.

The greater amberjack is actually quite slim, and as it grows older, it becomes proportionally more so. Compared to an older fish, a small (less than 16 inches long) greater amberjack is quite chunky.

For safety's sake, let's be redundant and remind you that the amberjack has spines. On the greater amberjack, there are seven spines in the first dorsal fin, and the second fin has two spines and 29 to 35 soft rays. The anal fin has one detached spine (sometimes covered by skin in large fish), an exposed spine, and 19 to 22 soft rays.

The greater amberjack is known to live in the eastern Atlantic Ocean from Africa's west coast to the Mediterranean; and in the western Atlantic from Brazil to Massachusetts. It is also found in the West Indies and around Bermuda. Because it looks like so many other fish species, the greater amberjack's exact range is unknown. It has been a popular gamefish with charter boats in the Carolinas and Florida for decades.

The Pacific amberjack, *Seriola colburni,* lives in the eastern portions of the Pacific Ocean from Ecuador up through the Gulf of California and as far north as Oceanside, California. It is slightly smaller and somewhat chunkier than its Atlantic cousin, and as it grows, this difference is intensified, for the Pacific amberjack's dorsal and anal fin lobes become more elongated.

Most fly fishermen cast for greater amberjack in the Atlantic. A few fishermen in the Cabo San Lucas area of Baja California may occasionally take a fish that looks a little bit like a roosterfish without the unique dorsal fins. But knowledgeable anglers will identify it as one of fly-fishing's growing delights . . . the amberjack! *(See p. 99 for color illustration.)*

Lefty's Fly Pattern Recommendations

Usually an amberjack is cast to after it's been teased near the boat. The key to presenting the fly is to watch the pale brown line that runs at a 45-degree angle above and in front of the eye to below the jaw. Until the fish becomes excited, this stripe is hardly noticeable. But when the stripe turns dark brown, that's the time to deliver the fly.

An amberjack under 40 pounds will usually take a streamer fly four to six inches long, such as a Lefty's Deceiver. A small fly will rarely catch a big amberjack; you need something that looks like a substantial serving. A large popping bug (any color) that makes a lot of noise is perhaps the best choice to offer this giant. If you keep the popper moving, the amberjack thinks the bug is bigger than it is, due to the water disturbance. Fly hooks for amberjacks range from #2/0 to #5/0.

GROUPER

Fishing for grouper, with a fly line or in print, can be an intimidating proposition. The family Serranidae, the sea basses, includes more than 400 species — many too small to consider gamefish, and a few even too large! Also, many groupers live in waters so deep that they're inaccessible to fly fishermen.

What we're looking for, then, are grouper that live in shallow water, will readily strike a fly pattern, and fight hard at least some of the time. We concluded there were nine.

All nine of these species have the typical grouper body: deep and well rounded and a large mouth and fins. All species live in the Atlantic over rocky shores — off Florida, in the Gulf of Mexico, in the Caribbean, and around the Bahamas.

The grouper written about the most is also the biggest — the **jewfish**, *Epinephelus itajara*, (also known as the spotted grouper) weighs up to 700 pounds. But a jewfish of several hundred pounds slowly moves toward holes in the rocky bottom, and few fly fishermen will ever bring this fish to the boat. Smaller jewfish are readily available to the fly fisherman, however, and hit fly patterns eagerly and fight well. A jewfish can be distinguished from its relatives by its rounded tail and the irregular spots and bars on its sides. Its territory extends from North Carolina to Louisiana and down to Brazil.

The next largest fish is the **warsaw grouper,** *Epinephelus nigritis,* which attains a weight of a couple hundred pounds, and fights well. It is almost entirely dark, sometimes with a few white spots sprinkled on the sides, and is often mistaken for a black grouper.

The **black grouper,** *Mycteroperca bonaci,* is considerably smaller, rarely weighing more than 50 pounds or measuring more than three feet. It is distinguished by dark, rectangular blotches on the sides, and an irregular series of pale lines between these markings. This popular fish is found in abundance in southern Florida, its young often found very close to shore.

Some Florida fishermen call the **gag** a black grouper, but the gag, *Mycteroperca microlepis,* is uniformly gray and lacks the black grouper's rectangular blotches. The gag grows as large as the true black grouper but has a more northerly range; some gag are taken as far north as North Carolina and as far west as Louisiana.

The **red grouper,** *Epinephelus morio,* is also very common in southern Florida. This fighter can exceed three feet in length. Its distinguishing marks are the overall reddish coloration and the absence of an indentation between the membranes of the dorsal spines.

Another grouper sharing the same waters is the **Nassau grouper,** *Epinephelus striatus,* which is normally a foot or two shorter than the Florida red grouper. This popular fish is marked by a number of dark blotches and bands and a dark "saddle" just in front of the tail. As its name implies, the Bahamas are one of its principal habitats.

Three smaller grouper — the yellowedge, the yellowfin, and the yellowmouth — can cause some confusion on paper. The yellowedge grouper can be disregarded, because it's a deep-water fish that is rarely accessible to any angler.

The **yellowfin grouper**, *Mycteroperca venenosa*, reaches a length of three feet, has red spots and dark irregular blotches all over its head and body, and is identified by the yellow edge on its pectoral fins.

The **yellowmouth grouper**, *Mycteroperca interstitialis*, is a much smaller fish, rarely 20 inches long. It is uniformly brown with some lines and spots spread over the sides.

And, finally, the grouper with the odd name — **scamp.** *Mycteroperca phenax* is fairly common along the southern Atlantic and Gulf Coast state shores and is a popular source of food for many people there. The scamp is usually less than 30 inches long, its tail is curved slightly inward, and its body is light brown with small dark spots. Like all grouper, the scamp does itself proud fighting a hook and line.

A lot of names and species have been left out of this writing. If you know enough to know that, you probably know all you need to know about grouper anyway. The point is, from a fly-fishing standpoint, all these species of grouper exhibit the same baitfish predation behavior and are easy to catch, provided you get their attention with your fly. (*See p. 99 for color illustration.*)

Lefty's Fly Pattern Recommendations

Although the larger groupers live too far down for a fly fisherman to get at easily, smaller groupers, ranging in size from one pound to 12 pounds, live around coral heads in less than 10 feet of water. They will eagerly take the fly — and often keep it!

Popping bugs of any color are irresistible to a grouper. Any basic saltwater streamer fly, such as the Whistler, Lefty's Deceiver, Clouser Minnow, or Surf Candy, fished around these coral heads or in channels, will draw strikes.

JACK CREVALLE
Caranix hippos

The jack crevalle is a relatively common saltwater species. Like many other fish, it suffers a name crisis. Some insist on calling it crevalle jack or just crevalle. And there are a ton of nicknames, many of which it shares with other jacks, so the same nickname can mean a different fish in different locations.

Such confusion is certainly understandable, because six or eight members of the jack family Carangidae share the genus *Caranx,* and there may be two or three times that many jack species in all. For the purposes of this field guide, let's just say there are jack crevalle living wherever there is warm saltwater, and much of what's true about them is true of all their cousins.

The crevalle has an extremely blunt head and a large, very forked tail, similar to the head and tail on a dolphin. Just in front of the tail on the lateral line some of the scales turn into scutes, which isn't overly important to the fisherman — until he grabs a fish there. Experience (and that includes pain and bleeding) has taught fishermen to be careful. You can still grab the fish in front of the tail, but watch your hand (and the fish's scutes) at all times.

The second dorsal fin and the anal fin are higher in front than in back on the jack crevalle and its cousins, the horse-eye (*Caranx latus*) and Pacific crevalle (*Caranx caninus*) jacks. Both fins run from slightly behind the midway point on the fish's body toward the tail, tapering the full length. The fins are mirror images of each other, and when the fish is viewed from the side, these fins resemble wings.

A jack crevalle's front dorsal fin is much shorter than the second dorsal and anal fins, usually with eight spines. The pectoral fins are long and delicate, and often golden, as is the underside of the fish. Key identification features on the jack crevalle are a black spot on the back edge of the gill plates and two other black spots on the forward underside of the pectoral fins. (The Pacific crevalle also has these same black markings.) On the back, the fish is often bluish black or metallic green, and on the sides, often silver.

Jack crevalle are schooling fish that work baitfish near the surface of the water, often inshore and near reefs. Some people claim that huge, solitary jack crevalle live offshore, as demonstrated by record catches of crevalle ranging from 40 to 70 pounds. Most fly fishermen, however, will catch jack crevalle weighing 20 pounds or under, while a few 30-pounders are taken on the fly each year. Current saltwater fly-rod records at various tippet strengths are just over that 30-pound benchmark, the notable exception being a 44-pound fish caught on 16-pound-test leader. As for the horse-eye and Pacific crevalle jacks, the record weights are generally less than half those of the jack crevalle. Most of the record jack crevalle were taken off Florida coasts, but Costa Rica also boasts some, and Mexican shores were home to many of the IGFA record-sized Pacific crevalle.

The schooling characteristics of the jack crevalle make it a popular gamefish with anglers. If you catch one, you may catch several of them. Many experienced fishermen feel that the jack crevalle is, pound for pound, one of the toughest fighting fish out there in the ocean. And as Lefty Kreh once pointed out to me, any fish with a markedly forked tail is a very fast moving fish. If you're fishing crevalle, the strike will be quick and jarring, and the fight will be memorable. Or at least that is what an awful lot of the fish's fans have been saying for decades. *(See p. 123 for color illustration.)*

The jack crevalle is one of the toughest fish that swims. It is always on the hunt for something to eat. It has been my experience that it will take virtually any fly or popping bug that is not too large for it, with the exception of predominately yellow patterns. For some reason, I have never had much success on the jack crevalle with a yellow fly.

LADYFISH
Elops saurus

The ladyfish belongs to the same family as the tarpon but is much smaller. Experienced tarpon fishermen can tell a ladyfish from a small tarpon by the lack of a single, long filament ray in the dorsal fin and by the scales, which are very small, unlike those of a tarpon.

A ladyfish is long and lean, with a lower jaw that protrudes slightly beyond the upper one and a tail shaped like a deep, sideways "V." The pelvic and dorsal fins are at least midway back, giving the fish a sort of Concorde-jet look. The pelvic fin is slightly ahead of the dorsal fin, and the dorsal fin has no spines.

The fish is silvery, with a white belly and silver sides. Sometimes the belly takes on a yellowish hue, and the sides may have a bit of color. The back is generally gray green or greenish blue, and the dorsal and tail fins are dusky or dark gray.

Ladyfish travel in schools and prefer shallow water that is over a sandy or muddy bottom, and they can be caught from shore, around piers, and off bridges. Offshore anglers fishing for other species occasionally catch ladyfish, too. The fish is no lady when hooked, often running off good lengths of line, making several leaps in the process and sometimes skittering across the surface.

There are ladyfish in most of the world's warm-water oceans. At least three additional species of the genus *Saurus* are known, some of them growing considerably larger than the ladyfish living in Florida or Caribbean waters. Our *Elops saurus* is especially prevalent off the southern tip of Andros Island, where first-time saltwater fishermen sometimes mistake its silvery body for that of a bonefish.

The ladyfish is not generally recognized as a standard gamefish, and only those who have fished for it seem to know much about it. In his 1958 book, *Salt Water Game Fishes*, Edward Migdalski admitted that most of the ladyfish he had caught were 16 to 20 inches long and weighed just one to three pounds; this is still the case today. Just the same, most experienced fishermen who have caught tarpon and bonefish rate the ladyfish as a legitimate gamefish, capable of mean and significant battles.

There are no fly-rod records listed with IGFA for ladyfish, but under the all-tackle heading there are three species, including two not listed by the American Fisheries Society. One of those fish weighed 22 pounds. Occasionally, fishermen seeking other species of fish, using large baits or lures, will unexpectedly take a decent-sized ladyfish.

Interestingly, experienced ladyfish anglers recommend using a wire tippet, not because of the fish's mouth or teeth but because the long body rubs against the tippet and acts like a metal file. Nature seems to have given every fish some edge for dealing with sport fishermen.

Some consider the ladyfish an "alternate species" and not a destination gamefish. But no angler can truthfully say he has never gone looking for other species when the fish he was originally after spurned his offerings. So the ladyfish has saved many an otherwise fishless outing, and once hooked, provided pretty good sport besides.

What more can you ask? *(See p. 133 for color illustration.)*

The ladyfish was called a 10-pounder years ago, perhaps because it fought like one. It's a small fish, usually weighing no more than two pounds. The largest ladyfish I ever found were off Belize's Turneffe Island, during the 1960s. Schools of them weighed five pounds! They were like mad dogs when they tore into your fly.

The best flies are any small streamers that imitate baitfish, such as the Glass Minnow pattern, small Lefty's Deceivers, or a simple, all-white pattern with a little Flashabou or Crystal Flash in the fly. The best hook sizes are #1 and #2.

MACKEREL
Scomberomorus cavalla, Scomberomorus regalis, Scomberomorus maculatus

It's hard to talk mackerel with a fisherman who spends most of his time in freshwater. Saltwater fishermen are familiar with these fish and their many names, sizes, and color patterns, but for a beginner they can be confusing.

The most elementary bit of research will reveal 20 to 30 common names for different kinds of mackerel. Attempts at serious research, comparing scientific Latin names, will show that for a long while, biologists used different names for the same fish and are just now beginning to sort it out. Fishermen have had names for the mackerel they caught for many years, but the same names were used by other fishermen for other fish caught in other locations. Beginners have a right to be confused.

The only responsible thing we can do here is talk about the species fly-fished for and written about most often. That brings us to the **king** *(Scomberomorus cavalla),* **cero** *(Scomberomorus regalis),* and **Spanish** *(Scomberomorus maculatus)* mackerel. All three live in the Atlantic, from South America to Cape Cod, but the Spanish mackerel is somewhat more common in the Gulf of Mexico and the cero in the waters of the West Indies.

The king mackerel grows the largest, some say up to 100 pounds, although most caught are between two and 20 pounds. The king mackerel is noted for its lack of brilliant coloration. Its back is predominantly blue black or dusky, its sides silvery, and its belly white. The fish is marked by a lateral line that takes a real big dip about midway back. The cero has yellow or orange spots and lines along its sides and one darker stripe that runs the entire length of the fish. The first dorsal fin of both the cero and Spanish mackerel is white near the body and black on the leading edge. The Spanish mackerel's sides have bronze or golden spots that are larger than the spots of a cero. A young king mackerel has spots also but can be distinguished from a cero or Spanish mackerel by the shape of its lateral line.

All three mackerel feature sharply tapered, "V"-shaped tails, eight to nine anal and dorsal finlets on the back half of the body, and spines in the first dorsal fin. Comparing the exact number of spines and finlets can lead to positive identification, but noting the color patterns is quicker and easier. Keep in mind we're talking about just three species of many, and only the adults of these three. The young of many kinds of mackerel may look alike.

The king mackerel generally prefers to hang out in deeper water than the cero and Spanish mackerel do, but it should be noted that all these mackerel will follow baitfish that come close to shore. They generally like to bunch baitfish together in pods and then hungrily rip through them. Although it's easier to catch these three species of mackerel from a boat, fishermen can be highly successful from shore, especially around piers and similar structures.

Most Spanish, cero, and king mackerel caught with a fly rod weigh less than 10 pounds, but kings do tend to run larger, sometimes weighing 25 to 30 pounds. Every IGFA world fly-rod record for the king and Spanish mackerel comes from Florida waters; no one has yet posted a record cero of any size on any tippet. As for other mackerel, fly fishermen in Australia have caught narrowbarred (*Scomberomorus commerson*) weighing up to 50 pounds.

The mackerel is a popular fly-fishing gamefish because it readily strikes a fly and fights well.

Finally, it should be noted that juvenile mackerel of many species are routinely used as bait for catching bigger fish. That's something even a beginner can understand. (*See p. 99 for color illustration.*)

Lefty's Fly Pattern Recommendations

A mackerel has keen eyesight and usually feeds on small baitfish while it is swimming very swiftly through inshore waters. Streamer flies dressed on #1 or #2 hooks and imitating local baitfish are the best patterns. Because of the mackerel's sharp teeth, you need to use a 30-pound monofilament bite leader in front of the fly, or else use a three-inch length of #2 or #3 stainless-steel trolling wire as a bite leader.

MUTTON SNAPPER
Lutjanus analis

While there are at least 15 to 20 separate species in the snapper family Lutjanidae, the one most often caught and talked about is the mutton snapper, whose range is the Atlantic from Florida to South America. Occasionally, the fish will be found as far north as Massachusetts and as far south as southern Brazil, but it usually sticks to tropical waters. Because it sometimes swims much closer to shore than its cousins, it is more accessible to the fly fisherman than other snapper species.

A reason for including the mutton snapper in this book is its size, up to 25 pounds. While the IGFA records for mutton snapper taken on a fly rod are all in the neighborhood of 14 to 15 pounds, the open-class division includes several over 20 pounds. Another valid reason for the interest in the mutton snapper on the part of fly fishermen — to whom aesthetics matter — is that it is truly one of the most beautiful fish to be found in the ocean. Yet another is its superb qualities as a gamefish. However, as Lefty points out below, it is an extremely difficult fish to take with fly tackle, some say even more difficult than the permit.

The mutton snapper looks somewhat like a freshwater bass, with its elongated, somewhat pointed head, thick, tapered body, and relatively large tail. The tail is crescent-shaped — pointed, slightly forked, but not notched or "V"-shaped. As on the smallmouth bass, the upper jaw does not extend beyond the beginning of the eye. The fins are dark orange, the color of red brick, and much larger than those of the bass.

On the top of its head and on the sides, a mutton snapper is sort of olive-colored with a bit of yellow or orange mixed in, and along the sides and belly, orange is predominant. Pale blue horizontal lines on its head and body fade out as the fish gets older and becomes more and more orange. Because of this color change, the novice fisherman sometimes confuses a mature mutton snapper with a red snapper.

But there are ways to tell them apart. The red snapper at any age is a more uniform, true red; even the eye is red, while only the iris is red on the mutton snapper. The red snapper's belly is lighter than its back or flanks, unlike the belly of a mutton. But the easiest way to keep the red and mutton snappers straight is to catch one of each on the same day — not impossible, since they inhabit many of the same waters.

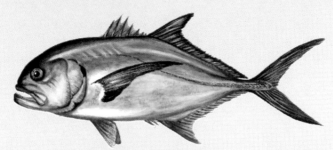

JACK CREVALLE (115)

MUTTON SNAPPER (121)

REDFISH (124)

SNOOK (135)

A more scientific method of telling a mutton snapper from its many cousins is to count its dorsal spines and rays. A mutton snapper has 10 dorsal spines and 14 rays, the rays making up the second dorsal fin and connected without a break to the first. By comparison, for example, the lane snapper has the same number of spines but just 12 rays, and other snappers have fewer or more. The rear section of the dorsal and anal fins on a mutton snapper is pointed, not rounded as on a lane snapper. And a mutton snapper also has a very distinct, black, oval spot on its flank, slightly more than halfway back on the body and above the lateral line. On our snapper's cousins, this spot is either lacking or located below or on the lateral line.

The mutton snapper is not easily fooled and it puts up a good fight. Fly fishermen who have been fortunate enough to take this fish on the fly say there's nothing at all sheepish about the mutton snapper. *(See p. 123 for color illustration.)*

Lefty's Fly Pattern Recommendations

Of all the flats' species, the mutton snapper is the most difficult I have ever tried to catch in all my years of fly fishing. The only time it seems vulnerable is when it is following a stingray, looking for food that the ray may have flushed out. In my opinion, the best fly pattern to use is a crab pattern, the Del Brown Crab Fly perhaps being the most successful.

REDFISH
Sciaenops ocellata

The redfish is a saltwater fish on the comeback trail. Fortunately for the fly fisherman, there are more of them available now than there were just a few years ago. Considering that this species has an expansive saltwater territory stretching from

New Jersey all the way to Mexico, that's quite an amazing comeback. A lot of people are responsible for this comeback, but it is primarily the Gulf Coast Conservation Association (based mainly out of Texas and Louisiana) and the sport fishermen in Florida who really led the way.

When the redfish (sometimes called red drum or sea bass) was approaching extinction across its U.S. range, these groups and others like them fought to protect it. Tougher laws were put on the books. Sport fishermen were required to release much of their catch, and commercial fishermen were severely limited in the number of redfish they could harvest. In a few cases, the sport and commercial seasons were actually eliminated, and even today in some U.S. waters commercial catches of redfish are still illegal.

Records and old photographs of redfish weighing up to 100 pounds attest to the proud memories of some redfish fishermen. For surf casters, the Outer Banks off North Carolina have traditionally been the source of the biggest redfish, and current IGFA records list fish ranging from 50 to 70 pounds caught there or nearby in the last 10 years. A few 90-pounders are still on the books, records dating from 20 years ago or more. Today's IGFA fly-rod records fill all six tippet categories. Three fish listed weigh 50 pounds or just under, but perhaps the most impressive records are a fish of almost seven pounds taken on 2-pound test and the one almost nine pounds taken on 4-pound test.

The redfish is elongated, its tail basically square. The snout is slightly rounded, and the upper jaw protrudes a little beyond the lower one. The species' back and sides are copper or bronze over silver or gray, the sides lighter, and the belly is white. A large black "eye spot" just in front of the tail provides the simplest, most immediate means of identification, although some fish have two or more spots. And for the scientifically inclined, the redfish has 11 dorsal spines in its first dorsal fin and 23 to 25 dorsal rays in its second. Like many saltwater fish, this species also has two anal spines, capable of causing injury to gloveless hands.

The redfish and the bonefish inhabit the same kinds of water, at least on occasion, but the redfish will work brackish water or even freshwater for brief periods of time. Experienced fly fishermen will take a boat to a tidal flat, spot redfish tailing, anchor up, wade to casting distance, and drop a fly in front of the feeding school. The fish often cooperate by feeding so intensely that they don't spook at the drop of the fly. Some Texas fly fishermen even swear that making the fly plop loudly actually attracts the fish. At any rate, the redfish does provide good sport under a variety of conditions, including murky water.

The redfish fights really well, not on the surface but in long powerful runs. A 10 or 20-pounder will allow a fly fisherman to see a lot of his backing, and not just once. On a good day a redfish angler should be able to catch fish weighing five to 15 pounds and between two to three feet long. Of course these are not world records, but it is extremely entertaining fishing. The fact that so many fishermen live near the U.S. southeastern Atlantic and Gulf coastlines explains, at least in part, why the fish is so popular — access!

The redfish's comeback is a success story that should warm the heart of any conservationist/fly fisherman. Good people can make good things happen. Still, that close call should also scare you, especially if you're new to the sport of fly fishing. A lot of other species have disappeared — maybe we just got unbelievably lucky with the redfish.

So enjoy your redfish fishing. Be glad the fish is there. Worry how long it will last and what other species are being fished right out from under you.

And after you worry, do your part to make a difference. *(See p. 123 for color illustration.)*

Lefty's Fly Pattern Recommendations

The redfish has become one of the most popular of all salt-water species found on warm-water flats. Many times it is likely to be found in murky waters or in flats filled with turtle grass, making it difficult for the redfish to locate the fly. Therefore, most redfish flies really must have some Flashabou or Crystal Flash, usually copper or gold.

A variation of the Clouser Minnow is the preferred redfish fly, usually dressed on #1 to #2/0 hooks. Another superb fly is the Bend Back, especially good to use when there are a lot of weeds in the water. Redfish also eagerly strike streamers of many colors, but tan, olive, brown, black, or a combination of these colors, with a little red or orange added, is best for streamer patterns.

ROOSTERFISH
Nematistius pectoralis

One of the most awe-inspiring sights in saltwater fly fishing is the seven long, thin dorsal fins of a roosterfish, raised and moving towards your fly. It's enough to make experienced fly fishermen freeze up and forget everything they've ever learned.

A last word about the fish's name. Do those raised seven finlets look like a rooster's comb to you? They don't to me. I've never seen a rooster with a comb like that in any barn I've ever visited. But let's move on.

Like marlin and sailfish, the raised dorsal fin of a roosterfish means it is chasing food — or it is ticked off by the pointed steel hook in its mouth. This fish puts up a terrific battle, and those who have caught it remember the battle as much as the take, which in itself is swift, sure, and strong.

In his popular book, *Fly Fishing in Salt Water,* Lefty Kreh wrote that the roosterfish was one of the toughest fish anywhere to be found. He also said, "Only a few have been taken on a fly, and it has to be regarded among the six top trophies a saltwater angler seeks." (I'll take that as a strong recommendation!) He explained that although it roams far out to sea, the roosterfish is also found right up in the surf chasing baitfish.

It is this sight of roosters going after baitfish that so fascinates fishermen: those unusual elongated, thin, flag-like finlets of the first dorsal ripping through the surf at incredibly fast speeds. A roosterfish will "greyhound" after small fish, leaping out of the water repeatedly or skimming along the surface for long distances, at speeds seemingly impossible for a fish of its size.

The roosterfish is shaped like an amberjack or crevalle, and is easily identified as a member of the jack family Carangidae. It has a slightly pointed head that rises abruptly to a high forehead. Also, its body is big and deep behind the gill plates and under the dorsal fins, and tapers sharply to a wide tail that is deeply forked, a tail built for speed.

But biologists were quick to notice the differences between the roosterfish and other members of its family, putting it in a genus by itself. (In fact, some scientists have given the fish its own family, Nematistiidae.)

The markings on the body of the roosterfish are a good way to distinguish it from its cousins. There are four distinct, dark bands that mark its side. The first band runs all the way from eye to eye, the second behind that, covering the back of the gill plates and running up over the top of the head. The back two bands both start underneath the front dorsal fin. The front one begins at a diagonal, parallel to the first two bands, and trails down the fish's side. The back band starts at the back of the first dorsal fin, descends like all the others, but then rakes back along the side of the fish in a nearly horizontal, dark band that extends clear all the way to the tail.

It's hard to imagine anyone, even on a first encounter, not recognizing a roosterfish. It is almost a uniform pearlescent color along the sides and belly, and the back is darker, either dark grays or greens — "creamy green," as Edward Migdalski described it in his popular volume, *Salt Water Game Fishes.*

The roosterfish lives almost exclusively in the western Pacific Ocean, from California to Peru, especially around Ecuador, Central America, and Mexico, including the Gulf of California.

Roosterfish IGFA records on a fly rod are 30-pounders, but the conventional gear listing includes several 60 and 80-pound fish, even one weighing 100 pounds. That's the good news. The bad news is that most of the records are old; few record-sized fish have been caught in the last five or 10 years. This could mean that the number of fish is decreasing and fewer fish are living long enough to reach tremendous sizes. It may also mean that these are world-class records that will take another 50 years to surpass. It may be worth your while to wonder and pay attention.

My only personal experience with the roosterfish was in Baja California, where I watched Paul Quinett, a prominent writer from Cheney, Washington, struggle with a 20-plus-pounder for a long, long time. During the battle, it wasn't too clear who was fighting whom. A roosterfish is no chicken — it's the bulldog of the Pacific.

Try it if you dare. *(See p. 133 for color illustration.)*

Lefty's Fly Pattern Recommendations

This tough, inshore brawler is one of the strongest saltwater fish you'll ever take on a fly rod. The usual way of catching the roosterfish is to tease it with an unbaited hook and then throw a fly. It has been my experience that the fish will take just about any streamer, but the most preferred fly patterns for a roosterfish are large popping bugs of any color.

SHARK

When most sportsmen think of fishing for shark, they envision fishermen endangering life and limb while wrestling monsters of the deep aboard big boats well off the coast. A fly fisherman, on the other hand, thinks of wading in shallow saltwater, stalking the basking fish with nothing between him but the fly rod and the fly.

There are over a dozen families of sharks and many species and subspecies. But from the fly fisherman's standpoint, two species are popular enough to warrant separate treatment: the blacktip and the lemon.

BLACKTIP SHARK
Carcharhinus limbatus

Blacktip shark abound throughout the tropical areas of the Atlantic Ocean, from Brazil to Massachusetts, and in the Pacific from southern California to Peru, and they are also common throughout the Caribbean and much of the Gulf of Mexico. They're often seen jumping clear of the water's surface well offshore or even in shallow water.

The blacktip's habit of feeding in shallow water makes it accessible to wading fly fishermen, and it's one of the few species that will readily strike a fly. No wonder it's singled out from all the world's sharks as a fly-fishing quarry. The blacktip is a willing competitor and puts up a great fight when hooked. And it's not monstrously big. A blacktip that is five and a half feet long will weigh around 65 to 70 pounds — small compared to many saltwater species pursued with a fly today.

As its name implies, this shark has black tips at the end of its pectoral and anal fins, as well as at the bottom lobe of the tail. The fish is gray overall, the back almost black and the belly close to white. Some blacktips have a bluish hue to the back and a little yellow on the sides.

The first dorsal fin of a blacktip is prototype shark. It is well up on the front half of the shark's body, not connected at all to the second dorsal fin, which is close to the tail. Biologists tell us that the gill slits are relatively small, but that's a bit of information which doesn't do you much good unless you wrestle with the shark or kill it.

The blacktip's close cousin, the spinner shark (*Carcharhinus maculipinnis),* looks a lot like it and, in fact, is also known as the large blacktip. It is larger than a blacktip, up to eight feet long, with a longer snout and proportionally smaller eyes. But it's easy to tell the two species apart: Big fish with long snout and small eyes equals spinner; smaller fish with blunt snout and larger eyes equals blacktip.

Fly fishing for the blacktip shark is not a new sport — it's been going on for years. There are no horror stories of fly fishermen being attacked by blacktips (or by any other species of shark, for that matter) while fishing. Blacktip excitement comes from this tried-and-true formula: a big fish that's within casting distance and willing to take the fly. When you add the rush of the fight, it's easy to understand why experienced saltwater fly fishermen are always looking for the blacktip shark anytime they're fishing for other saltwater species. (*See p. 133 for color illustration.)*

Lefty's Fly Pattern Recommendations

The blacktip and lemon sharks and other sharks that inhabit the shallows can be very exasperating fly-rod targets. Large sharks appear to be swimming slowly, but anyone who has poled a boat and tried to catch up to one knows it is actually moving rapidly across the flats. Any large shark (three feet or longer) on the flats is incredibly wary when it is in water less than three feet deep and will flee at the slightest disturbance. Boat noise and poling have to be kept quiet, and there should be no scuffing of feet in the boat during an approach.

These sharks have excellent hearing, but they do not see that well. For this reason, the best flies need to be brightly colored and should include strands of Flashabou or Crystal Flash. I have fly fished for sharks since the 1950s, and have become convinced that flies with red and orange, or red and yellow, or orange and white combinations, are the best producers. Large Lefty's Deceiver-type flies work well. A dozen strands of the flash material should extend a half-inch or so beyond the end of the fly's wing.

Popping bugs attract sharks, but you must present these flies differently. The mouth of a shark is far back from the nose, so when a shark rises to take the popper, the nose or front part of its body tends to push the fly away. Therefore, when a shark is swimming towards you, you should not present and retrieve the fly in front of its nose. Besides, it will often not see a fly presented directly in front of it. Rather, you should present and retrieve the fly at its side, close to its eye. If this is done properly, the shark will strike with a sideways movement of its head.

LEMON SHARK
Negaprion brevirostris

The other popular shark with saltwater fly fishermen is the lemon shark.

Like the blacktip and spinner sharks mentioned in the previous essay, lemon sharks are members of the Carcharhinidae family of sharks, commonly called requiem sharks, at least by biologists. To most fishermen, this means absolutely nothing. So what? Well, because they're *family*, they share some common characteristics. For one thing, they're small

LADYFISH (117)

ROOSTERFISH (127)

BLACKTIP SHARK (130)

LEMON SHARK (132)

fish. There are no great whites in the family. No makos. No blues, or leopards.

A mature lemon shark may reach 11 feet long, but it doesn't have a heavy build and won't weigh as much as distant cousins of the same length. And, like family, they'll hang out in shallow water. They will also strike a fly, and no one knows why, so they share that trait with their close relatives, the blacktips. For a fly fisherman, that's critical.

But the biggest reason for the lemon shark's popularity with fly fishermen is the abundance of the baby lemon shark on saltwater flats, like baby tarpon. Since the fish is born in early summer anywhere in the Atlantic or Pacific where the water is warm, by mid-summer or early fall there are little fish everywhere — and there will be one, two, and three-year birthdays to celebrate.

Sharks are known for their gluttonous appetites, and the young lemon shark holds up this family tradition well. It loves to eat and will strike a fly in shallow water. The young often swim in small schools and can be stalked like . . . bonefish!

Sport is where you find it, and the lemon shark provides it for fly fishermen off Florida's shores, off the coast of Ecuador, throughout the Caribbean, in shallow waters of the Gulf of Mexico, and up the Eastern Seaboard as far as New Jersey. And when tidal action makes their prey more readily available, the fisherman's odds go up.

Experienced fly fishermen who have caught many species of fish say they like fishing for the lemon shark because they can rig their tackle for the size they see. One day there can be 10-pounders, another day, 20-pounders. They "match the hatch" not with the fly but with the tippet!

Identifying a lemon shark is easy. It's yellowish-brown overall and has a slightly wide and round snout. The two dorsal fins are approximately the same size and shape, unusual for sharks (or for most fish), and the front dorsal doesn't have that menacing look you see in man-eating-shark movies. The teeth can be useful in identifying the lemon shark, but I think that's getting entirely too close for practicing catch-and-release.

Do you really need to know anything else about lemon sharks? OK, they're not dangerous. Trust me. *(See p. 133 for color illustration.)*

Lefty's Fly Pattern Recommendations
See Blacktip Shark.

SNOOK
Centropomus undecimalis

Snook are one of the most easily identified saltwater fish. Their backs are a darkish brown, black, gray, olive, or bronze, depending on their habitat and feed. The sides are predominantly silver, and the belly white. A snook has a very prominent black lateral line that runs from behind the top of the gill plate, down the middle of the body, and right through the tail. There's even a short extension in the "V" of the tail where the black line continues.

Some people call snook saltwater pike. While this is definitely not scientific, the shape of the snook's head is indeed similar to that of a pike's. The snook has a protruding lower jaw, a mashed-down snout, and the look of a predator. But from the gill plate back, any similarity to the northern pike ends. The snook's body is full and compact, the tail lobes are rounded, and the two dorsal fins are separated by a gap, the rays in the front fin basically soft spines. A note of caution: The gill plates of snook can cut your hands or shear your leaders, as many have learned through painful experience. There is also an anal spine, so be careful.

The snook lives in warm tropical waters, from Florida to Brazil in the Atlantic. Almost all the IGFA records for snook on a fly rod come from Florida waters. Bill Barnes, owner of Casa Mar Lodge on the Rio Colorado (which separates Nicaragua and Costa Rica on the Caribbean side) took a 26-pound snook near his lodge on 16-pound-test leader in 1980. On conventional gear, anglers have taken snook weighing from 25 to 40 pounds in Florida waters and in Costa Rica.

The snook in the Pacific, from Baja to Peru, are black snook (*Centropomus nigrescens*). Although IGFA lists no records for this species, that's not to say a whole lot of folks aren't fishing for, catching, and having fun with this fish. The Pacific snook's following just doesn't match the following of the Atlantic fish, which probably means there are a lot more snook in the Atlantic than there are in the Pacific.

Most fly fishers catch the snook in fresh or brackish waters. A snook will cruise from the tropical saltwater into freshwater, looking for food and passing a lot of *Homo sapiens* along the way. It is a fairly accessible fish.

Biologists tell us that the snook stops feeding once the temperature of the water drops below 60 degrees F., so a bit of cold weather can definitely close down the fishing. But in southern Florida, Costa Rica, and other parts of the Atlantic and Pacific tropical areas, this doesn't happen very often. That's good for the snook and good for the fisherman.

If you've never fished for this species, you should know that many folks have, and they always go back for more. Guides in Costa Rica make a living taking people fishing for snook, and even go after it on their own on their days off. The snook fights extremely well. The strike is jolting, the runs breathtaking. This fish looks strong, and it is.

Believe every word you hear about the snook's reputation. Go fishing for it yourself just as soon as you can. (*See p. 123 for color illustration.*)

Lefty's Fly Pattern Recommendations

The snook is one of the top-rated fly-rod fish of the shallows, perhaps because it acts so much like a largemouth bass. Both fish like to hide behind logs, under bridges and pilings, and around brush piles; and they take the same kind of flies — popping bugs and streamers. Some favorite streamer flies are the Seaducer (a very old bass pattern), Lefty's Deceiver, the Punch series of flies, and the Clouser Minnow. Many anglers use flies with weedguards, since the fish hides in fly-snagging structures such as mangrove roots.

Because the snook's gill plates have a sharp cutting edge, a 10 to 12-inch bite leader is recommended. I prefer a 30-pound, monofilament bite leader; wire seems to deter strikes, especially in clear water. To get more action from a popping bug, use a Non-Slip Mono Loop.

SPOTTED SEATROUT
Cynoscion nebulosus

Talking about seatrout can get confusing. First of all, most folks doing the talking are talking about spotted seatrout, although there are two lesser-known seatrout, sand and silvery, that inhabit some of the same waters as their popular cousins. Completely unrelated, however, are sea trout (two words), which refers to a seagoing brown trout in Europe, Iceland, and to a lesser degree, the northeastern coast of the U.S., Canada, Argentina, Chile, and New Zealand.

The territory of spotted seatrout (one word) ranges from New York south to Florida and all over the Gulf of Mexico. Generally found in shallow estuaries, searching for shrimp, seatrout are more common south of Virginia. All the IGFA world records come from Florida and Texas, and on a fly rod, they range from eight to 12 pounds. Fishermen in Florida and

Texas often refer to the fish as specs, speckled trout, trout, or even sea trout.

Spotted seatrout do look a little bit like a freshwater trout, so that's undoubtedly where the common name comes from. The resemblance does stop, however, with the general body shape, tail formation, and black spots on the body, tail, and dorsal fin. A spotted seatrout has saltwater self-defense systems that freshwater trout lack. For one thing, there are two big canine teeth in the front of their mouths, and spines on the back and on the belly. Specifically, the first dorsal fin has 10 spines, and the second dorsal fin has one. There are two spines located in the anal fin.

Coloration of a spotted seatrout is largely silver on the sides and belly, the upper sides taking on a bluish tinge, and the back blue or gray. It is generally spotted above the lateral line, and on its second dorsal fin and tail. The fins are pale or yellow green.

Scientists tell us that while the spotted seatrout usually lives in shallow estuaries, it will feed at any level in the water column. And while it prefers shrimp to other food, it's been known to strike any number of baits or lures. The fish has a maddening habit of staying in shallow water when winter temperatures drop, and a good many seatrout die every winter. No one knows why they don't just swim for open water and warmer temperatures.

Adding to the bits and pieces of a biologist's nightmare are these facts. Spotted seatrout are members of the drum family, Sciaenidae, but very few members carry that family name. Specs and weakfish share *Cynoscion* as their genus name, but neither species is a weak fish. They both have soft tissue mouths, which will rip easily, so horsing either species with a stiff rod and ultra-stiff leader is not an option. If you want to fish for spotted seatrout (more about weakfish later), especially with a fly rod, you're going to have to match the fish's anticipated weight with rod, line, leader, and fly. That's un-doubtedly why so many enjoy fly fishing for this fish. *(See p. 93 for color illustration.)*

Lefty's Fly Pattern Recommendations
Two types of flies are very effective on spotted seatrout. This fish (and the weakfish, or gray trout) seems to show more interest in surface motion or noise than any other species, with the exceptions of the smallmouth and largemouth bass, so a popping bug is a good choice. The color of the bug is unim-portant; you only need to be able to cast the fly easily and make noise with it on the retrieve. On calm waters, a bug that makes just a little disturbance can be effective, too.

The other pattern that works well is a brightly colored streamer dressed in fluorescent yellow, chartreuse, orange, or red. Lefty's Deceivers, Clouser Minnows, Bend Backs (where there's a lot of grass in the water), and standard bucktail stream-ers are all producers.

A combination of patterns can be deadly at times. For ex-ample, using about 10 inches (no longer, to avoid excessive tangling) of 15-pound-test leader, attach a Clouser Minnow, Bend Back, bucktail streamer, or any fly with flash to your lead fly, a popping bug. You can pop the bug to attract the trout, and when the fish sees the dangling fly, it will nearly always strike.

STRIPED BASS
Morone saxatilis

The striped bass is a sportsman's fish, ready to strike a fly and fully capable of growing to 60 pounds. Most striped bass caught with a fly rod weigh 25 pounds or less, but that doesn't affect the striper fisherman's fervor. The fact that an angler does connect occasionally with a 40 or 50-pound monster keeps most anglers in a state of excited anticipation.

The striped bass is easily identified. It has a relatively long head and a pointed snout, and is usually green, blue, or black on the back, silver on the sides, and white on the bottom or belly. The most distinguishing physical characteristics are the seven or eight thin, black, horizontal stripes from the gill plate to the tail. One line falls right on the lateral line and three or four lines run parallel above it. The three lines below do not extend as far back as the others.

The striped bass has two prominent dorsal fins. Both are shaped like triangles, but as anyone who has ever taken a geometry class can tell you, not the same kind of triangles. The front dorsal fin is more menacing and has eight to 10 spines. The second dorsal fin, entirely separate from the first, features 10 to 13 soft rays. And the anal fin has three spines right on its leading edge, and seven to 13 soft rays.

The striped bass is found in the Atlantic, the Pacific, coastal rivers, estuaries, and many freshwater impoundments in between. It is anadromous but spawns in freshwater streams off the Atlantic Coast in the spring. Off the Pacific Coast, it moves into freshwater streams in the fall, winters there, and then goes back down into deltas and freshwater tributaries to spawn.

Its range is impressive. The striped bass can be found, always close to shore, from the Louisiana shoreline east to Florida and up to New England, and from Southern California to Washington State. The heaviest concentrations on the East Coast are from South Carolina to Massachusetts, and on the West Coast in the San Francisco Bay area, although the fish is not native to the Pacific.

It's in the impoundments of the southeastern states where the striper develops some truly maniacal followers. The explanation is simple: the striper gets big, often over 20 pounds, and it's usually an off-season fish, always a bonus.

The striped bass has responded well to various preservation programs. If there is a textbook example of how proper fishery management can pull a fish species out of serious decline, this fish is it. In the 1980s, striped bass had virtually disappeared from the East Coast due to overfishing. However, with recent good management of the fishery, there are now more striped bass in these waters than there have been for decades.

And in watersheds such as reservoirs or other landlocked bodies of water, the abundant population of stripers in recent years has had a lot of help from humankind. For many years, stripers spawned upstream, leaving their eggs in the reservoir. Because striper eggs must drift with the current in order to become fish, development was extremely difficult, since a reservoir has no current. Therefore, to preserve the species, many states began to raise these young stripers in hatcheries and then plant them in the reservoir as fingerlings or catchables. And eventually — though biologists had to get real creative to make it happen — some of these hatchery fish began to reproduce on their own.

As a result of this ingenuity and hard dedicated work, there are striped bass virtually all over the place — Alabama, Texas, Oklahoma, Utah, and elsewhere. And the number of sites with impounded striped bass will probably continue to increase, given the fish's potential size and its reputation for being a voracious feeder. The striped bass has been planted in impoundments in order to rid them of trash fish, and, with supporting trash fish, in sterile sites to create a sport fishery where none existed before.

Saltwater fly fishermen say the striped bass is one of the best gamefish available today. The reason being that the striper hits extremely hard, fights well, and makes long runs, especially when hooked while in shallow water. That's certainly a dream come true for any fly fisherman.

Since the fish is found in such a wide variety of habitats, generalities about its coloration or spawning habits or about the best month for fishing become somewhat meaningless. It all depends. So wherever you fish, ask around — there's bound to be a striped-bass fishery relatively close by. Go find them already! *(See p. 93 for color illustration.)*

Lefty's Fly Pattern Recommendations

Flies for the striper fall into two categories. For stripers up to about seven or eight pounds, smaller flies dressed on hooks from #2 to #2/0 will do the trick. For larger fish, much longer, bulkier flies are needed. Hooks for these flies range from #2/0 to #5/0.

The favorite fly for most anglers who take striped bass in salt or freshwater is the Lefty's Deceiver. An all-white Deceiver with a chartreuse topping or a pattern that imitates local baitfish is usually best. The Clouser Minnow is another excellent fly. The size of the metallic eyes that you use will depend upon how deep you want the fly to swim. The universal choice in this pattern, by far, is a white underwing with a chartreuse upper wing and a good bit of pearl Crystal Flash or Flashabou between the two. Popping bugs are also effective, as is the Whistler series developed by Dan Blanton specifically for stripers.

Special note: In an effort to catch large striped bass, some anglers have developed outlandishly large fly patterns that are very hard to cast. There was no need to do that. *The Lefty's Deceiver can be modified to produce a fly that is at least a foot long and appeals to large fish.* To increase the wing length, first dress the pattern with long strands of FisHair or Ultra Hair, and on each side, tie in a number of saddle hackles. Build a large collar of bucktail or whatever material you choose, and add big Mylar glue-on eyes at the head. The result is a huge fly that can be cast even on a rod as light as 10-weight.

TARPON
Megalops atlantica

Tarpon are one of the most popular and sought-after saltwater gamefish with fly rod and a fly. Everyone has seen pictures of fishermen with a 100-pound tarpon alongside the boat, grinning (the anglers, *not* the fish) like Cheshire cats, and releasing the fish. That's as it should be. This ancient fish deserves a little respect, after all the years of catch-'em-drag-'em-to-the-dock-and-take-pictures mentality they've endured.

And while fishing for these incredible 100-pounders (and seeking to eclipse the current IGFA fly-rod records of 187 and 188-pounders) gets all the press and certainly keeps a lot of guides busy, it's baby tarpon that many fly fishermen actually prefer to go after, including Lefty Kreh. A textbook definition of baby tarpon is a youngster 20 pounds or under. However, knowledgeable fishermen, like Lefty, frequently catch baby tarpon that weigh well over 20 pounds.

Tarpon are spawned in large numbers — millions of eggs per female — and they need about seven years to reach full maturity. An adult tarpon is usually about four feet long and weighs around 100 pounds. That means that during that period of seven years that the young tarpon is developing with all of its buddies, there are a whole lot more two-foot tarpon around than six or seven-foot tarpon. And besides, handling an 8-weight rod (an ideal weight for baby tarpon) all day is a whole lot more comfortable than hefting the 12-weight rod that's needed for the big fish.

Tarpon are found in warm tropical waters from Florida to Brazil, in the Bahamas, throughout the Gulf of Mexico to Venezuela, and in the coastal waters of West Africa. From a behavioral standpoint, there is considerable variety among the tarpon species. Some fish remain residents in the waters of their birth their entire lives.

Others — particularly the mature, very large fish — join migrating herds, or pods, which make annual migrations over a wide area of the ocean. This is particularly evident in the Gulf of Mexico, where huge pods of tarpon arrive each year in the Lower Keys in the spring months and work their way northward up both coasts of Florida during the summer months, some then continuing west toward Texas and Mexico, others moving northeast toward the East Coast of the U.S. and the water around Bermuda.

Resident tarpon can be found year-round (particularly near clusters of mangrove islands), and fishing simply improves as the migratory fish move into the area.

Describing a tarpon is relatively easy because the fish is so physically distinctive. It's much longer than it is wide or deep, and its sides are nearly vertical. The last ray in the dorsal fin is greatly elongated, stretching almost back to the tail. The fish is also noted for its huge and heavy scales with rough edges as well as a "bait-bucket" mouth that's hard as nails. Tarpon also have an extremely forked tail.

More specifically, the lower jaw of a tarpon protrudes forward and up, and the upper jaw closes down on top of it. The eyes are well forward and close to the top of the head, which is very flat. The back of the fish is usually dark gray or blue (which is noticeable when the fish roll), as is the dorsal fin, with 12 to 16 soft rays, and the tail. The sides are brilliant silver, unless the fish has been in brackish water, where it may take on a slightly brownish or yellow color.

Tarpon have an air bladder, or false lung, which they can fill by rolling on the surface and breathing in oxygen. Scientists and fishermen postulate that by having air available to them, tarpon can live in brackish water almost totally devoid of oxygen, which allows them to live their lives almost completely free of major predators who require oxygenated water. This may explain why they've been around for millions

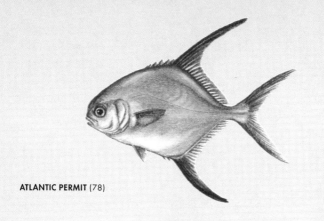

ATLANTIC PERMIT (78)

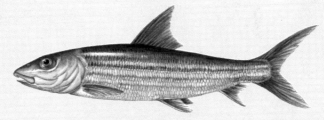

BONEFISH (95)

GREAT BARRACUDA (106)

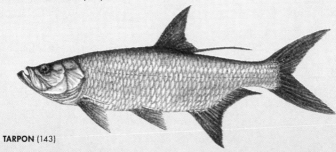

TARPON (143)

and millions of years. And since most brackish water is relatively shallow, this also explains why fly-fishing guides and fishermen can easily locate and cast flies to this great gamefish. It's highly doubtful that any other saltwater fish as big can be taken with a fly rod in such shallow water. That really explains the fish's popularity; like many other gamefish, the tarpon is readily accessible.

There's also the issue of fighting characteristics. Tarpon are mighty fish. When describing their encounters with tarpon, many fishermen speak in terms of runaway freight trains. There have even been recorded instances of people being killed by tarpon. Usually, it's been a situation when a big fish still full of energy was brought into a small flat's skiff. I saw a video once of a tarpon that was yanked sideways into a boat just as it leapt clear of the water. Fly fishing for tarpon should be exciting. But don't go overboard and let that fish inboard! (*See p. 145 for color illustration.*)

Lefty's Fly Pattern Recommendations

To stand on the bow of a small flats skiff and see a six-foot-long tarpon approach is awesome. Many anglers aren't even able to cast at first. For large tarpon, quite heavy tackle is needed, such as a 10 to 12-weight line and rod, and flies from #4/0 to #2/0 (#3/0 is pretty standard). Of course, smaller tarpon can be fished with lighter tackle. Tarpon have no teeth, but their mouths are very abrasive, so a 30 or 40-pound monofilament bite leader is recommended for smaller fish, an 80 to 100-pound for giant tarpon.

Every tarpon fisherman has firm ideas about which flies are best. The fact is that in clear waters, such as the Florida Keys, a whole host of fly patterns produce. I suggest you carry the following patterns to cover all situations: Red and White, Stu Apte Tarpon Fly, Black Death, Cockroach (if you only carry one fly, this is it), and the Del Brown Crab Fly.

TUNA

When considering fly fishing for tuna, you have to limit your field. There are many species — some better sport, some more accessible, some just willing to hit a fly. Here are brief introductions to the four species all anglers should know about.

BLUEFIN TUNA
Thunnus thynnus

If you use your imagination, you could say the bluefin tuna is sort of blue all over. There's no marked color contrast anywhere on the fish, just steel blue on top, with some green shimmer, fading down the body to a silver gray. It does have some yellow in its finlets, and the front, square-shaped dorsal fin is collapsible. On its sides, a younger bluefin tuna has vertical lines, made up of white spots and streaks.

This fish is known for its incredible size — on conventional gear, a bluefin weighing just shy of 1,500 pounds was taken off Nova Scotia in 1979 — and in its vast migrating range; tagged fish have been caught as far as 5,000 miles from where they were tagged.

Anglers have a chance at the bluefin in the Pacific and the Atlantic oceans at various times of the year. It is best to consult a specialized travel agent or refer to the various saltwater fishing magazines for details on the best bluefin tuna venues at any particular time. All the IGFA fly-rod records on this fish weigh in a range of modest sizes — just 14 to 32 pounds — and all of these fish were caught off the shores of New Jersey and New York State. (*See p. 149 for color illustration.*)

Lefty's Fly Pattern Recommendations
See Blackfin Tuna.

BLACKFIN TUNA
Thunnus atlanticus

Blackfin tuna are found in the western Atlantic from Cape Cod to Brazil, but all the world-record fish taken on a fly rod have been caught either in Florida waters or off the Bahamas. Although these record fish range from 25 to 35 pounds, most fly fishermen will catch blackfin tuna that weigh between five and 10 pounds.

There are subtle differences between this small, dark tuna fish of warm tropical waters and the other tuna species and albacore. The finlets behind the second dorsal and anal fins are dark; many other species have a little yellow on these finlets. A blackfin tuna has long pectoral fins that reach back almost as far as the start of the second dorsal fin. Light bars alternate with light spots on the sides, and the back is dark, as are the tail and all the fins except the first dorsal.

Identification is relatively easy — black fins, blackfin tuna.

Lefty's Fly Pattern Recommendations

The most important thing to remember when fishing for blackfin, bluefin, and yellowfin tuna is that these fish have incredible eyesight. Unless the water is slightly roiled, which is rare, they will not accept a fly on a heavy leader. Often, 10-pound-test is the largest you can use that will still draw strikes.

Sometimes large flies will work well on tuna, but usually flies shorter than four inches do best. On many occasions, blackfin especially will gorge on baitfish no more than three inches in length. If the fly you are presenting isn't doing the job, cast a smaller, sparsely dressed fly on a thinner tippet.

Fly patterns that work well on most tuna are glass minnow imitations, small, lightly dressed Lefty's Deceivers, or Clouser Minnows dressed with slim wings of some transparent wing material such as Ultra Hair.

COBIA (102)

DOLPHIN FISH (104)

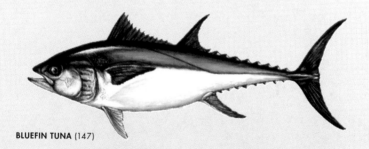

BLUEFIN TUNA (147)

WAHOO (152)

YELLOWFIN TUNA
Thunnus albacares

A mature yellowfin tuna is easily identified by its super-extended second dorsal and anal fins, and by its yellow fins. A golden or iridescent blue stripe runs back along the fish's sides from the eye to the tail; it is sometimes faint. As is the case with many species, these identifying characteristics may be hard to find on an immature fish.

The yellowfin is less migratory than a bluefin, and smaller, too, though it is much larger than a little tunny or blackfin tuna fish. On conventional gear, yellowfins have been taken at weights of 200 to almost 400 pounds, and on a fly rod, from 40 to 80 pounds, in spots like Mexico, Venezuela, and Bermuda. They are fish of tropical waters worldwide, providing great sport off the Hawaiian and Australian coasts, for example.

When you decide to go for yellowfin, you need to know where you're going before you get there. Some lodges cater almost exclusively to yellowfin tuna fishing, but you should shop around carefully and make a few long-distance calls to check the references provided. For something as important as a yellowfin tuna on a fly rod, you don't want the lodge, guide, or time of year to be a problem. Do your homework.

Lefty's Fly Pattern Recommendations
See Blackfin Tuna.

LITTLE TUNNY
Euthynnus alletteratus

The little tunny, yellowfin, bluefin, and blackfin tuna are all members of the mackerel family, along with the albacore and wahoo. In terms of body shape and tail configuration, the little tunny obviously has more in common with an albacore and the other tunas than with a wahoo, and the little tunny's colors and markings make it easily distinguishable.

For one thing, the sides of the little tunny are very distinctive, with spots like fingerprints between its pectoral and pelvic fins. And the fish has vermiculations on its upper side above a well-defined lateral line, from the tail to about midway through the front dorsal fin.

The little tunny lives only in the Atlantic, from New England to Bermuda, over to South Africa, and up to Great Britain. It prefers warmer water. All the IGFA records for little tunny come from Florida waters, the weights between 13 and 18 pounds. The little tunny is, in fact, little, but numerous and eager to strike a fly.

Strike forth yourself.

Lefty's Fly Pattern Recommendations

Fishermen often refer to little tunny as albacore or Fat Alberts. The fish search coastal waters for small baitfish like bay anchovies. The trick to catching little tunny is to race to where you can see them leaping from the water as they grab the small baitfish. Then throw a fly in their midst.

The best fly I have ever used — the one I now use exclusively — is a Clouser Minnow. I dress the fly sparsely and paint the metallic eyes silver with a black pupil. Although bucktail works, I prefer a transparent wing material such as Ultra Hair. The upper wing is usually pale green or blue, but in slightly roiled waters, a chartreuse upper wing seems to draw more strikes. I normally tie the lower half of the wing in a smoke or white color. I then tie in a few strands of pearl or pink Crystal Flash or Flashabou. In the past few years, the albacore population has exploded along the East Coast and now provides some of the top fishing for fly rodders from New England to Florida.

WAHOO
Acanthocybium solandri

Wahoo are bad dudes. Solitary, growing to a length of up to six feet, and attaining a weight well over 100 pounds, they're called "the cheetahs of the sea," capable of speeds above 50 miles an hour. Reportedly, most are caught as incidentals to attempts for bigger species, such as marlin and sailfish.

There's no big problem in identifying a wahoo. The body is long and lean and the snout long and tube-like. The back of the fish is dark blue, and there are light-blue tiger stripes from dorsal fin to belly all down the sides. Some say the colors are almost electric, or iridescent or sparkling.

A wahoo's reputation comes from its runs. Many fishermen swear this fish can make multiple 100-yard runs, and it's an unwise angler who puts a thumb down to slow the unwinding of line on the reel. Around the Bahamas and Bermuda, starting in the spring and early summer right up through early fall, anglers will fish for wahoo for weeks at a time, to their captains' delight. And to their clients' delight, wahoo on the line occasionally make spectacular jumps into the air, so everyone is happy.

Seriously — and these paying customers are — the people who fish for wahoo know that they're going for a very special fish. Although they are widely dispersed in all oceans, wahoo don't school up much once they reach maturity. Seeing two to five big fish at a time is the norm, but enticing one of them to take your fly is a real challenge. A challenge of equal proportions is what to do once a wahoo is on the line. Fly fishermen who have met these challenges report that a wahoo on the fly is well worth the time, effort, and money that must be expended to land one.

If you get a wahoo to the boat, you may notice that the gills look more like those of a marlin than those of the mackerel/

tuna family to which the wahoo belongs. Its body shape is more like that of billfish, too. Wahoo have a mouthful of teeth; 45 to 64 on the upper jaw and 32 to 50 on the lower jaw. They can move both jaws, and the teeth are compressed. That all translates into instant death for wahoo meals, mangled baits, and mangled fingers if someone gets careless.

The front dorsal fin on a wahoo is long, composed of 23 to 27 spines. The second dorsal and the anal fin are both quite short, with just about half as many soft rays. The lateral line is very visible, starting behind the eye at the gill plate and running straight back the fish's side until a point opposite approximately midway back in the first dorsal fin. At that point it takes a big dip down toward the middle of the fish's body and continues back toward the tail in wavy lines. It's unique and a means of positive identification, regardless of any individual fish's specific color patterns.

The wahoo provides sport for fishermen all over the globe, anywhere there's warm saltwater. On a fly rod, world-record fish weighing between 17 and 46 pounds have been taken in Panama, Australia, and Bermuda. The 2-pound-test tippet class is open and may stay open for a long time.

If some have found a way to take a 40-pound wahoo on a fly rod, what's to stop others from catching the 50 or 150-pounders that are taken with conventional gear? Looks like the popularity for fly fishing for wahoo is just beginning. (*See p. 149 for color illustration.*)

Lefty's Fly Pattern Recommendations

You will need a wire bite leader in front of the fly when fishing for wahoo, since their teeth are extremely sharp, as Dennis points out. Like tuna, they have exceptional eyesight, so light, thin wire no longer than five inches is suggested.

Throwing streamer flies at a wahoo is frequently unsuccessful. However, if you chum the fish near the boat by tossing many small baitfish into the open sea, the wahoo will more readily take a fly. A Lefty's Deceiver (or similar baitfish imitation) with a few strands of silver or pearl Crystal Flash or Flashabou helps entice the wahoo into striking.

WEAKFISH
Cynoscion regalis

Weakfish aren't. Weak fish, that is. Weakfish are a saltwater gamefish species closely related to spotted seatrout. Unfortunately, some people interchange the names. They shouldn't. Weakfish have far more spots, and those do not extend onto the dorsal fin or tail like they do on spotted seatrout. And there's more. The spots on weakfish seem to line up in wavy diagonal lines, in either black, olive, or bronze color combinations. All of this shows up on the upper sides of the weakfish, mainly above the lateral line, which is fairly high on the fish's side to start with.

Weakfish are popular because they're accessible. They spend summers as far north as Massachusetts, with heaviest concentrations from Delaware to New York. Winters, they move south, with heaviest concentrations present between Florida and North Carolina. The IGFA world records show that. In the section listing the biggest weakfish caught on a fly rod, the locations listed are Delaware Bay; Cape May Court House, New Jersey; Chesapeake Bay, Virginia; and Lloyd Point, Long Island. The biggest fish weighed under 15 pounds, and most of them were closer to 10 pounds.

But weakfish like to school up and move in over shallow sandy bottoms. That makes them accessible in large numbers, to lots of people in boats, off piers, and even in the surf. They are found in sounds, inlets, bays, channels, and saltwater creeks. They'll swim into river estuaries, but not freshwater itself. They have their preferred haunts, and they stick to them. They're not nearly as migrational as many saltwater fish, so weakfish fishermen know where to find their quarry.

Add that to the fact that they're extremely good eating, and you begin to see why they are so popular. The East Coast of the U.S. has a big concentration of people living near the ocean. It seems the weakfish are doing their part to reproduce and live in enough areas, and in enough numbers, to satisfy a good part of the people who fish for them.

Still, there's the matter of the name. Why weakfish? It has to do with a soft tissue membrane in the mouth. It's extremely fragile, and hook-ups with this membrane rip loose with very little pressure. Consequently, someone's great-grandfather started calling these fish weakfish; not for their fighting characteristics, but as a means of describing how carefully one had to set the hook and combat these special fish.

The weakfish has a very long head. The mouth is proportionately large, the snout tapered. The lower jaw extends past the upper one. It has two big canine teeth in its mouth, like its relative, the spotted seatrout. There are 10 spines in the first dorsal fin. The second dorsal extends farther and features a single spine and 26 to 29 soft rays. It's usually somewhat dark, mixed with a little yellow.

The belly is light colored, the tail broad, mildly forked and olive in color, with some yellow. The spots mentioned earlier look like they're thrown on the upper back half of the sides. Some call it a peppered look.

Overall body coloration varies from region to region, and sometimes fish to fish, but *generally,* weakfish are dark colored on the back, some shade of green or blue. The sides are blue, green, or purple, interspersed with copper or gold.

Don't start looking for a peacock in the sea. All these colors are muted, and the fish's general appearance is that of a fairly dull coloration. However, closer examination of a fresh caught weakfish will reveal some or all of the colors mentioned here. And like most of nature's creatures, the weakfish is, in its own way, quite beautiful.

In short, the weakfish is all that a fly fisher could hope for: accessible, willing to strike a fly, and reasonably sized.

As mentioned before, weakfish aren't. They're strong, in many, many ways. *(See p. 93 for color illustration.)*

Lefty's Fly Pattern Recommendations
  See Spotted Seatrout.

INDEX

A FIELD GUIDE TO FLY FISHING